Created in the Image of God

Princeton Theological Monograph Series

K. C. Hanson, Charles M. Collier, D. Christopher Spinks,
and Robin Parry, Series Editors

Recent volumes in the series:

Paul G. Doerksen
*The Church Made Strange for the Nations:
Essays in Ecclesiology and Political Theology*

Lisa M. Hess
Learning in a Musical Key: Insight for Theology in Performative Mode

Jack Barentsen
*Emerging Leadership in the Pauline Mission: A Social Identity
Perspective on Local Leadership Development in Corinth and Ephesus*

Matthew D. Kirkpatrick
*Attacks on Christendom in a World Come of Age: Kierkegaard,
Bonhoeffer, and the Question of "Religionless Christianity"*

Michael A. Salmeier
*Restoring the Kingdom: The Role of God as the "Ordainer of Times
and Seasons" in the Acts of the Apostles*

Gerald W. King
*Disfellowshiped: Pentecostal Responses to Fundamentalism
in the United States, 1906–1943*

Timothy Hessel-Robinson
*Spirit and Nature: The Study of Christian Spirituality
in a Time of Ecological Urgency*

Paul W. Chilcote
*Making Disciples in a World Parish: Global Perspectives
on Mission & Evangelism*

Created in the Image of God

Understanding God's Relationship with Humanity

NICO VORSTER

Foreword by Fika J. van Rensburg

PICKWICK *Publications* · Eugene, Oregon

CREATED IN THE IMAGE OF GOD
Understanding God's Relationship with Humanity

Princeton Theological Monograph Series 173

Pickwick Publications
An Imprint of Wipf and Stock Publishers
199 W. 8th Ave., Suite 3
Eugene, OR 97401

www.wipfandstock.com

ISBN 13: 978-1-61097-223-9

Cataloging-in-Publication data

Vorster, Nico.

   Created in the image of God : understanding God's relationship with humanity / Nico Vorster ; foreword by Fika J. van Rensburg.

   xiv + 182 p. ; 23 cm. —Includes bibliographical references.

   Princeton Theological Monograph Series 173

   ISBN 13: 978-1-61097-223-9

   1. Theological anthropology. I. Van Rensburg, Fika, 1951– II. Title. III. Series.

BT701.3 .V65 2011

Manufactured in the U.S.A.

Contents

Foreword

NICO VORSTER IN THIS BOOK EXPLORES FROM A REFORMED PERSPEC-
tive various topics related to theological anthropology. The book focuses on some of the key and much debated themes that pertain to the
relationship between God and humanity. The book is divided into two
main sections. Part One revisits the Reformed doctrine of the *imago
Dei*, as well as other Reformed doctrines that are of decisive importance
for a theological anthropology. Part Two utilizes this revisited reformed
approach, as well as other theological and philosophical insights, to address some of the most crucial ethical issues that concern anthropology
and the cohesive functioning of society today.

In Part One, Vorster persuasively argues that Reformed theology
ought to cleanse itself of some of the literalist Augustinian errors that
permeate the reformed understanding of creation and sin, specifically
the doctrines on evil and original sin. He shows how the Augustinian
legacy still permeates reformed theology, in spite of the fact that Calvin
and other reformed theologians have provided some corrections to the
Augustinian errors. Vorster indicates that much work still needs to be
done within the reformed tradition on the implications of evolution for
theology.

Part Two stresses the need for an integrative approach to the three
fundamental human values of dignity, freedom and equality. Vorster
purports that contemporary human rights discourse discards the importance of the natural environment for human survival, because it
is engrained in the anthropocentrism of modernity. Third generation
rights will have to receive greater emphasis, combined with globally enforced environmental laws. Otherwise dignity will not be maintained.

He convincingly argues that some first generation rights (such as
the right to free trade, freedom of movement, the freedom to practise a
profession of your choice, and the freedom to possess private property)
at times will have to be limited in favour of certain key second and third
generation rights. He indicates this as probably the only way to protect

the environment and natural resources, and views global warming and the risks to security that accompany it as the single greatest threat to human dignity today.

For Vorster, therefore, it is of utmost importance that liberalism rethinks its stance on the relationship between freedom and equality, and these two values must be made compatible. If this does not happen, the growing global inequality will be a time bomb ready to explode. To this end Capitalism ought not to enforce the principles of competition, maximal profit and self interest in all spheres of life, but respect the importance of the human relations that underlie all transactions. Capitalism should take social justice, equity, fairness and the preservation of the natural environment seriously.

This book of Nico Vorster illustrates that the strength of Reformed theological anthropology is that it is able to correlate the values of dignity, equality, and freedom with each other. Vorster does not ground these values anthropocentrically in the autonomy of the individual bearer of rights, but within a broad cosmological framework that respects the immanent principles underlying every created sphere of life. Due recognition to God's creative actions and his divine will—this Vorster agues convincingly—gives human relationships cohesiveness and equilibrium.

Our global society that lives on the edge of chaos should embrace this cohesive understanding of rights and values.

Fika J. van Rensburg
Dean of the Faculty of Theology
North-West University
Potchefstroom, South Africa
February 2011

Preface

THIS BOOK IS WRITTEN FROM A REFORMED PERSPECTIVE AND EXPLORES various topics related to theological anthropology. The aim of the book is not to provide an exhaustive treatise on theological anthropology, but to focus on some of the key and much debated themes that pertain to the relationship between God and humanity. Part One revisits the Reformed doctrine of the *imago Dei*, as well as other Reformed doctrines that are of decisive importance for a theological anthropology. Part Two utilizes the theological approach to anthropology explicated in Part One, as well as other theological and philosophical insights, to address some of the most crucial ethical issues that concern anthropology and the cohesive functioning of society today.

The first part is entitled "Theological Perspectives on Human Nature, Sin, and Atonement." It deals with the theological meaning of the ambiguous yet theologically important concept of the *imago Dei*, the mystery of evil, the much-debated concept of original sin, and the rationale behind the reformed doctrine on atonement.

Chapter 1 first discusses the significance of the concept of the *imago Dei* for a theological anthropology. Though the *imago Dei* is rightly regarded as a biblical theme that is of crucial importance for the explication of a theological anthropology, it is also characterized by some ambiguity. For instance: why is *sélém* (reflection) and *děmût* (copy) used interchangeably in Genesis 1? Does the *imago Dei* in Genesis 1 denote a physical image or is it a relational concept? What is the relationship between the *imago Dei* and God's command to rule? What is the effect of sin on the *imago Dei*? Is there some continuity between the Priestly understanding of the *imago Dei* and the Christological content that some of the New Testament epistles give to the concept? Chapter 1 states that Genesis 1 assigns an "open" meaning to the concept which makes further reflection on the nature of the *imago Dei* possible. A purely protological understanding of the concept is therefore insufficient. The New Testament imbues the *imago Dei* with a Christological and eschatological sense that is essential for a correct understanding of the concept, as well as for the development of a theological anthropology.

In his famous work "Evil and the God of Love" John Hick suggests that the "Augustinian" type of theodicy is based on an outdated worldview and ought to be replaced by what he calls an "Irenaean" type of theodicy. Chapter 2 examines Hick's claim by analysing the views of the three main theological exponents of the Augustinian paradigm on evil namely Augustine, John Calvin and Karl Barth. It suggests that Reformed theology rethinks its linear concept of time and considers the possibility that the Fall could be an event in time with an eternal significance that works both "backwards" and "forwards." Chapter 2 concludes that weaknesses in the Augustinian paradigm can be resolved from within, and that no need exists for Reformed theologians to replace the Augustinian paradigm with an alternative Ireneaen paradigm that jeopardizes key Scriptural teachings on creation and sin.

Chapter 3 discusses the Reformed doctrine on original sin. First, it focuses on the way in which Calvin modified Augustine's doctrine of original sin. It puts forward the hypothesis that the main differences between Calvin and Augustine can be attributed to different theological aims. Augustine developed his doctrine of original sin against the teachings of the Manicheans and Pelagians, whereas Calvin shifted the focus to knowledge of God and the self. Calvin understood original sin noetically as religious and moral blindness—whereas Augustine viewed sexual concupiscence as the main principle of original sin. Augustine went to considerable effort to explain that sin does not find its origin in God. God foresaw the Fall but did not compel it. Calvin located sin in God's eternal decree. Augustine, furthermore, understood the transmission of original sin biologically, whereas Calvin ascribed it to God's eternal permissive will. These differences culminated in a different understanding of the meaning of Jesus' virgin birth. The chapter concludes by discussing the relevance of Calvin's noetic approach to original sin and the ways in which his noetic approach can help to cleanse reformed-theological anthropology from the literalist errors of Augustine's biological understanding of original sin.

There is a wide disparity of opinion about the most important event in the Christian faith. Chapter 4 examines the Reformed doctrine on atonement through penal substitution and the importance thereof for a theological anthropology. The first section briefly discusses the historical origin of satisfaction theory, while the second section outlines some criticisms levelled against satisfaction theory since the Reformation. Questions directed at the Reformed doctrine of satisfaction are the following: Can the guilt of one person be imputed to another person? Why does God need a blood sacrifice to placate His anger? Is the notion of a Substitute not an affront to individual responsibility? The final part of the chapter attempts to answer these criticisms by reflecting on the multi-dimensionality of the images used in the New Testament for the atoning work of Christ, the illegality of sin, the relationship between God's love and righteousness and the meaning of Christ being both priest and sacrifice.

Subsequent upon Part One dealing with some key theological concepts in Reformed theology that pertain to the relationship between God and humanity, Part Two, entitled "Ethical Perspectives on Dignity, Equality, and Freedom," utilizes this theoretical framework as well as other theological and philosophical insights to deal with important ethical issues related to what I consider to be the three main aspects of the status that God bestows on the human, namely human dignity, freedom and equality. The relationships between human dignity and non-human dignity, equality and freedom, economics and freedom, and equality and otherness are scrutinized.

Chapter 5 addresses the current ecological crisis and the implications thereof for a theological anthropology. This chapter states that modern society requires an ethical and legal discourse that directs itself to the whole of creation, rather than only to human society's dependence on its natural environment or its survival. A conception of dignity is therefore needed that will be able to relate human and non-human dignity. A multi-relational understanding of dignity is proposed, based on a reading of the Genesis narrative as well as other major themes of Scripture. It entails that human and non-human dignity ought to be understood and evaluated in terms of the dignity of the entirety.

One of the major challenges for modern society is to balance the conflicting interests of freedom and equality in the public domain. Chapter 6 attempts to provide a Christian perspective on freedom and equality that might help to reconcile some of the conflicts between freedom and equality that are likely to arise. The first section discusses the significance of religious ethics for social justice, the second section attempts to provide a conceptual framework for freedom and equality from a theological perspective. The third section offers a societal framework within which conflicts between freedom and equality can be resolved. The conclusion arrived at is that freedom and equality are compatible values as long as they are used in a conceptually correct manner which upholds the inherent principles governing societal processes.

Chapter 7 focuses on theology and otherness. It investigates the manner in which the Apartheid and Nazi theologies were instrumental in sacralising the history of a specific group by creating origin myths, by idolising the ingroup, by defining the outgroup, by providing racist ideologies with rituals and symbols, and by creating final utopian solutions. The theological doctrines that were used are characterised by certain common features, such as a collectivist anthropology, the identification of the church with an ethnic group, the view of history as a source of revelation, and the appropriation of myths. The chapter concludes with the observation that the modern global environment is particularly vulnerable to racism. It is therefore important for Christianity to clearly identify the common characteristics of pseudo-racist theology and to educate its adherents on the difference between authentic theology and pseudo-theology, so that they will not fall prey to destructive forms of religion that encourage racism.

The 2008 implosion of global financial markets reiterated the need for the reform of modern capitalism and renewed reflection upon the relationship between economics and freedom. Milton Friedman was one of the most influential economists of the twentieth century. Many of the neo-liberal views that he advocated were adopted in the 1980s by Western countries such as Britain and the United States. Chapter 7 analyses Friedman's views on politics, economics, and freedom. The first section discusses his perspectives on the relation between capitalism and freedom, the nature of markets, his understanding of equality and of the social responsibility of business. The second section attempts to provide an immanent ethical critique based on Friedman's separation between economics and ethics, his concept of the market, his views on freedom and equality and the implications of his economic doctrine for human identity. The third section offers some key Christian-ethical principles that may help to reform modern capitalism.

The book concludes with concise final remarks regarding anthropological issues that require further reflection.

Acknowledgments

THIS BOOK WOULD NOT HAVE REALIZED WITHOUT THE SUPPORT OF A number of influential people in my life. First, I would like to thank the National Research Foundation of South Africa as well as the Theological Faculty of the Northwest University for their financial support of this project. A special word of thanks to Prof Nicholas Meihuizen and Christien Terblanche who were responsible for the language editing of the text. Part of the research of this project was done at the Karl Ruprecht University of Heidelberg. I would like to express my gratitude to Prof Michael Welker who made the visit possible and enabled me to utilize the facilities at the Karl Ruprecht University. I am also grateful for the enlightening conversations with him and Prof Klaus Tanner. Pickwick Publications, especially Charles Collier, deserves special mention. Their management of the publication process was highly professional. Lastly a word of thanks to my wife Christelle, and my parents Koos and Hannatjie, who supported me throughout this project. I value their support. May this book serve the glory of God!

PART ONE

Theological Perspectives on Human Nature, Sin, and Atonement

1

Image of God

Introduction

CHRISTIAN THEOLOGICAL TRADITIONS ALMOST WITHOUT EXCEPTION take the concept of the *imago Dei* as point of departure for its doctrine on the human being. However, there is little agreement amongst theologians on the precise content and meaning of the *imago Dei*. The human being's image-bearing qualities have for instance been located in free will, intellectual and rational capacities, moral nature, self-consciousness and the immortal soul, emotional characteristics that distinguish persons from animals, a self-transcendent nature, outer appearance, being God's representative on earth and a relationship with God.[1] These different interpretations are mainly due to the fact that the Priestly creation narrative gives a vague definition of the human being as an image-bearer. The multivalented use of the concepts *ṣelem* (reflection) and *děmût* (copy) especially leads to confusion and speculation. Old Testament scholars agree that the concept of the *imago Dei* only appears in the Priestly parts of Genesis 1–11, which is dated relatively late. According to some the *imago Dei* can therefore not be regarded as a central concept in the Old Testament.[2]

However, the validity of this statement depends on the content ascribed to the concept. If the *imago Dei* is essentially understood as a description of the inherent characteristics of the human being, as postulated by Irenaeus, Philo and Gregorius, the concept is not of central importance in the Old Testament. If it is a relational concept that

---

1. Cf. Towner, "Clones of God," 343.
2. N. Macdonald, "Imago Dei and Election," 304.

3

indicates the nature of the human being's relationship with God, or if it indicates the way in which the human being represents God on earth, it can be stated with confidence that the *imago Dei* is of crucial importance for a theological anthropology. Towner[3] rightly indicates that all biblical anthropology is ultimately theological anthropology that defines the human being in terms of his relationship to God. Although the reference to the human as image of God seldom appears in the Old Testament, the Old Testament understands the nature of the human being in terms of a relationship with God.

It should furthermore be kept in mind that systematic theology's interest in the *imago Dei* is largely due to the Christological content that the New Testament ascribes to the concept. The New Testament authors agree with the Priestly narrative's description of the status of the human, but they also expand the concept of the *imago Dei* by relating it to Christ and applying it eschatologically to the life of the church. According to Grenz[4] the concept of the *imago Dei* is a key motive in New Testament Christology. The New Testament authors use it to explain God's salvation-historical work in the human being from the beginning to the end. The dogma of the *imago Dei* therefore has important implications for a theological anthropology, hamartology and Christian understanding of salvation.

The purpose of this chapter is to provide an outline to a theological anthropology by focussing on the concept of the *imago Dei*. The central theoretical argument is that the Priestly narrative purposely ascribes an "open" meaning to the concept of the human being as image of God which makes further theological reflection possible. The *imago Dei* should therefore not only be understood from a protological perspective, but the Christological and eschatological content that the New Testament gives to the concept is crucial for the understanding of the concept and the development of a theological anthropology. At the same time the New Testamentical definition of the human's image-bearing can not be properly understood without the protological foundation of the image-bearing in the Priestly narrative. One can never speak of the human being as image of God without taking note of God's original aim with the creation of the human.

3. Towner, "Clones of God," 305.

4. Grenz, "Jesus as the Imago Dei," 626.

The Imago Dei in Protological Perspective

Genesis 1:26–28 offers different interpretative possibilities regarding the human's image-bearing qualities. The image can be connected to the representation of God, based on Gen 1:26. The interchangeable use of *dĕmût* and *selem* makes it possible to qualify this representation as a reflection of God's virtues (*dĕmût*) or to seek it in ontological and physical characteristics that the human shares with God (*selem*). *Dĕmût* appears in the Old Testament 21 times and comes from a Hebrew root that indicates reflection or copy. *Selem* can be translated as likeness. The word is used 17 times in the Old Testament and mostly indicates physical representation.

The image-bearing can also, based on Gen 1:27, be linked to man's creation as male and female. If verses 26 and 27 are read together, the image can be sought in the fact that the human, like God, simultaneously leads a singular and plural existence. It is furthermore possible, on the basis of verse 28, to understand the image as a combination of man's creation as male and female and his mandate to rule over creation. Each of these possibilities have been followed in history.

Representative Views

Based on the words *dĕmût* and *selem* in Gen 1:26–28, Ireneaus distinguished between the human as image of God in a natural sense (*imago*) and a super-natural sense (*similitudo*). The *imago* then indicates the human's natural capacity for ingenuity and freedom, while the *similitudo* indicates a super-natural likeness of God. According to Irenaeus the *imago Dei* suggests that it is the destination of the human being to ultimately become part of the divine nature.[5] The problem with Irenaeus' understanding is that it shows a strong Gnostic influence. His notion that the human is a physical image of God—or that the human can take part in the divine nature—is contrary to the anthropology of the Old Testament, which maintains a distinction between God and human beings. The prohibition that the Second Commandment places on depictions of God, as well as the Old Testament's association of such activities with heathen practices, are clear indications of this.

---

5. Vorster, *Kerk en menseregte binne 'n regstaat*, 282.

Several Old Testament scholars follow Von Rad in explaining selem in terms of the ancient Near Eastern Imperial ideology. Von Rad[6] states this theory as follows:

> Just as powerful earthly kings, to indicate their claim to dominion, erect an image of themselves in the provinces of their empires where they do not personally appear, so man is placed upon earth in God's image as God's sovereign emblem. He is really only God's representative, summoned to maintain and enforce God's claim to dominion over the earth.

According to this view the priestly writers took over the Imperial ideology and extended it to all of humanity.[7] Bird,[8] though, indicates that the Old Testament's use of selem does not support such an interpretation. It should furthermore be kept in mind that the Old Testament places a lot of emphasis on God's personal and continous involvement in creation. Although the Old Testament rejects any form of pantheism that removes the distinction between God and his creation, it does not accept a form of deism that seperates God and creation in an absolute manner either. Von Rad's view does have merit in the sense that the priestly creation narrative and other parts of the Old Testament do assign an imperial status to the human, but then not in the exact terms of Near East Imperial ideology.[9]

According to Brunner[10] the Priestly narrative uses the concept of the *imago Dei* to express humankind's formal structure of being. The human is a "reflection" that points to "Someone else."[11] The human is created by God as a being that stands opposite to God. This relationship is characterised by the fact that God reveals himself to the human in the Word and that He at the same time gives the human the rationality to receive his Word.[12] The human was not only created by God, but was created in and for God. The essence of the human's creaturely nature consists in a free self-determination that finds the basis of his existence

6. Von Rad, *Genesis*, 60.

7. N. Macdonald, "Imago Dei and Election," 304.

8. Bird, "Male and Female He Created Them," 140.

9. Cf. Psalm 8.

10. Brunner, *Man in Revolt*, 92.

11. Ibid., 96.

12. Ibid., 103

and knowledge in God Himself.[13] The human is a free and responsible being who receives the gift not only to exist, but to be free to exist. The human is not a once and for all completed being like the animal, but a being who can develop through self-knowledge and self-determination.[14] The question is whether Brunner's foundation of the image in free self-determination does justice to the text of Gen 1:26–28. The dialectical distinction between I and Thou on which his argument of free self-determination is based, is a modern anthropological-philosophical concept that is foreign to the ancient Priestly text.

The decisive question is: Why does the Priestly narrative use *děmût* and *ṣelem* interchangeably? It is possible that the weaker expression, *děmût*, is used in parallel to the stronger expression, *ṣelem*, in order to define the human's image-bearing of God in a strong, yet nuanced, manner. The human is a representative of God, but in the sense of reflection, not physical similarity. The human is not a precise copy of God, but reflects something of God's kinglike rule in ruling over creation.[15]

In opposition to Brunner and the classical church fathers, Barth rejects the idea that the human's image-bearing can lie in any inherent qualities or formal structure of the human. This would entail that the human's image of God could be distinguished from his relationship with God. Barth also rejects the notion of a possible natural point of contact between God and the human, because this would deny the extent of God's saving grace in Christ.[16] Since humans were created with Christ in mind, they were created in the image of God. According to Barth[17] the human can never be understood in isolation from fellow humans and God. The human is a being that lives in a state of interaction. The nature of these relationships is determined by God's covenant. In his exegesis of Gen 1:26–28 Barth especially focuses on the plural form used for God, and the fact that verse 27 links the human's image-bearing to the creation of male and female. Based on this he comes to the conclusion that the human's image-bearing pertains to the I-YOU relationship in

13. Ibid., 96, 97.

14. Ibid., 97, 98.

15. Cf. Jenni and Westermann, *Theologisches Handwörterbuch*, 560–61.

16. Jónsson, *Image of God*, 69.

17. Barth, *Church Dogmatics* III/2, 319.

the Divine being which is reflected analogically in the human.[18] As the speaking I in God's being stands in relation to the Divine Thou, so God stands in relation to the human, whom He addresses as his partner. This I-Thou relation is continued in the creaturely relation between male and female.[19] In the same way as the relationship in the Divine Being is characterised by differentiation and community, the human, who has been created as male and female, is a being who lives in juxtaposition and conjunction. The human is a relational being who leads a dialectical existence as male and female, *id* and *ego*, as an individual but also a collective being, egocentric but also self-transcendent.[20]

Barth's understanding of the human's image-bearing as a relational concept had a great influence on the Protestant tradition.[21] However, his interpretation of Gen 1:26–28 is not without problems. The question is, as in the case of Brunner, whether Barth really respects the original intention of the Priestly author. Does Barth not perhaps manipulate the text in order to construct his dialectical anthropology from it?

Like Barth, Jürgen Moltmann ascribes a relational content to the *imago Dei* by linking Gen 1:26 and 27. However, he tries to avoid Barth's dialectical approach in his definition, and avoids any hierarchical distinctions of dependence amongst beings that could be founded in the cultural mandate. Moltmann seeks the image in the singularity and plurality of God that can also be found in the human. As the relationship within the Trinity is characterised by differentiation in relationships and relationships in differentiation, the human existence is also characterised by pluriformity.[22] Although Moltmann acknowledges that it is not the intention of the Priestly narrative to develop a doctrine of the Trinity, he is of the opinion that the text is open for it.[23] He bases his view on the plural and singular terms that can be found in Gen 1:26 and 27:

> Gen 1:26: Let us (plural) create man in our image (singular), our representative

18. Cf. Barth, *CD* III/2, 245.

19. Durand, *Skepping, mens en voorsienigheid*, 156.

20. Towner, "Clones of God," 345. Jónsson, *Image of God*, 73

21. Cf. Jónsson, *Image of God*, 67.

22. Moltmann, *God in Creation*, 223.

23. Ibid., 224.

Gen 1:27: As image of God He created man, male and female (plural) He (singular) created them.

According to Moltmann[24] the singular image of God in verse 26 corresponds with the internal plurality of God, while the plural reference to the human as male and female in verse 27 corresponds to the Divine singular. Although Moltmann's relational foundation of the image in verses 26 and 27 possesses elements of truth, his exegesis is problematic for two reasons. Firstly, it seems like forced exegesis to give a Trinitarian content to the Divine plural in 1:26. Moltmann's dogmatic Christian explanation of the text certainly does not agree with the Priestly writer's original intention with the concept, with the result that the unique protological content that the Priestly writer assigns to the image is not taken into account. Although some Old Testament scholars are of the opinion that the Priestly writer merely uses the plural of majesty in Gen 1:26, most commentators agree that the reference here is to a Divine consultation. There are several references in the Old Testament to God consulting with the heavenly beings around his throne.[25] It is possible that the Divine plural is used in verse 26 as a counter measure to prevent the human's image-bearing being linked too directly to the being of God. According to Von Rad[26] such an interpretation is probable because the same technique is used in Gen 3:22.

The second problem with Moltmann's exegesis is that he separates the human's creation as male and female from the mandate to rule in verse 28. According to him the mandate to rule is the result of the human's image, and is not part of the image itself.[27] He understands the human's creation as male and female solely on the relational level, while ignoring the biological implications thereof.[28] In this way he artificially gives the image-bearing of the human an egalitarian content without addressing the problems that arise from the mandate to rule in verse 28.

---

24. Ibid., 217–18.

25. Cf. Towner, "Clones of God," 344. Von Rad, *Genesis*, 59. 1 Kgs 22:19–23, Job 1:6—2:6, Psalm 82.

26. Von Rad, *Genesis*, 58

27. Moltmann, *God in Creation*, 224.

28. Cf. Welker, *Creation and Reality*, 67.

Phyllis Bird and Michael Welker read Gen 1:27 in conjunction with verse 28. According to Bird[29] sexual differentiation and biological reproduction belong to the core of the human's image-bearing. Genesis 1:27 not only describes a social relationship between male and female, but also a biological relationship. Bird motivates her view by referring to the general androcentric nature of the Priestly texts that especially comes to the fore in the constitution of the genealogies and cultic prescriptions. The biological core of the human's image-bearing becomes clear when the human's creation as male and female is read together with the culture mandate to rule. Humans should reproduce and multiply in order to rule. Under "rule" (*rádâ* and *kābash*) she understands a violent subjection. Precisely in the multiplication and rule through violent subjection the human's relation to the image is seen.

The value of Bird's analysis lies in the fact that she takes the biological side of the human's image-bearing into account and reads verse 27 and 28 in conjunction. She does not attempt to explain away the hierarchical distinctions that underlie Gen 1:28, as Moltmann does. However, it is an open question whether her understanding of the text is not determined by a feminist agenda. The violent and power driven foundation that she gives to the human's image-bearing is not in agreement with the broader context of the Priestly creation narrative. Although the words *rādâ* and *kābash* indicate violent subjection in other parts of the Scripture, it appears in the Priestly narrative within the context of paradisal harmony. Botterweck and Ringren[30] rightly show that *rādâ* is used in Genesis 1 within the context of conservation as an act that serves the benefit of creation as such. This does not mean to say that *rādâ* and *kābash* have no violent meaning within the priestly narrative, but rather that the context softens the content of these words to such a degree that they cannot be interpreted rigidly. The mandate to rule is furthermore given within the context that the human is created as image of God. This indicates that the mandate cannot be interpreted as establishing a right to exploitation, since the human's image-bearing implies that the human has to act in a way that mirrors divine responsibility.

29. Bird, "Male and Female He Created Them," 229.
30. Botterweck and Ringgren, *Theological Dictionary of the Old Testament*, 336.

Michael Welker offers a more nuanced perspective on the relationship between verse 27 and 28. According to Welker[31] the concept "creation" in the creation narratives indicates the construction and sustenance of associations of interdependence between different creaturely spheres. The culture mandate presupposes a hierarchy of relationships between humans and animals. Although human and animal share a mutual environment, animals are beings of a lower order that live in subordination to humans. The Priestly narrative is clear that animals can in no way enjoy a higher status than humans. The human as image of God stands over and against animals. At the same time the Priestly creation narrative states that mutual interests do exist. Although the relationship between human and animal is hierarchical in nature and contains a violent element, it also has a positive side. Firstly, humans live in communion and solidarity with animals in the sense that humans and animals share the same environment. Secondly, humans should, analogous to the imperial ideologies of the ancient East, rule in a responsible manner over animals.[32] The culture mandate thus stresses that the creation should be conserved in accordance with its complex structures of interdependence, while the interests of human's are considered as of prime importance. Humans may use violence to conserve and protect, but not in a manner that destroys community. Welker's explanation of the image is attractive because he seriously considers the message of the text and does not try to enforce modern philosophical categories on the text. He furthermore takes into account both the biological and relational elements in the image, as well as the hierarchical references in the words *rādâ* and *kābash*.

A Possible Hypothesis

In the light of the preceding discussion the following hypothesis can be stated with regard to the protological content of the *imago Dei*: Gen 1:26–28 gives a careful and open meaning to the human's image-bearing. On the one hand the text aims to relate God and human beings to each other through the concept of image. On the other hand the text instates checks and balances that safeguard the radical distinction between God and human beings. As a result the human cannot be re-

31. Welker, *Creation and Reality*, 13.
32. Ibid., 71.

lated to God too closely. These checks and balances are instated through the interchanging use of *děmût* and *ṣelem* in verse 26 and the reference to the heavenly consultation in verse 26. The text does not attempt to give an exact content to the image. It for instance does not provide an ontological explanation of the human's structure of being, but rather gives a broad description of the implications of the *imago Dei* for human existence. This "open" approach of the text creates the possibility for further reflections on the meaning of the *imago Dei*.

Genesis 1:26–28 clearly understands the *imago Dei* as a relational concept, but it also provides the concept with a definitive hierarchical and biological meaning. The Priestly creation narrative deals with the relationship between God, the human and the creaturely creation, and the resulting calling that the human receives. God and humans are related to each other, but are also distinguised from each other—humans and animals are related to each other, but are also distinguished from each other. The relationship between God, human and animal is characterised by community, but is at the same time hierarchical in nature. Contrary to animals, the human is created to live in relation to God. The human represents God on earth, but is not God. This representative nature immediately implies responsibility towards God. God's virtues must be reflected in the manner in which he relates to the creaturely spheres in God's creation. Precisely what these virtues entail is left open for further reflection.

Just as there is a hierarchical element in the relationship between God and the human, the human's relationship to the creaturely is hierarchical in nature. Humankind's creation as male and female on the one hand indicates a biological potential to multiply and rule, and on the other hand the social capacity to communicate and cultivate. The human is superior to animals. This is illustrated by humankind's capacity for self-conciousness and communication. However, his right to rule over the creaturely sphere is not synonymous with unlimited power or the right to exploitation. It is a rule accompanied by duty. Rule through exploitation implies that the ruler wants to exert his own will at the cost of the inherent rights of the sphere over which he is ruling. Rule that is accompanied by duty presupposes that the ruler is aiming for an overarching goal that is more important than his own immediate interests.[33]

---

33. Cf. Pannenberg, *Anthropology in Theological Perspective*, 80.

Genesis 1 clearly deals with a rule that is accompanied by duty. In their rule humankind should be responsible towards the Creator. They should conserve the associations of the different creaturely spheres and should never destroy the communion between the different spheres.

Sin and Image

Within mainstream Christian theology there is, with a few exceptions, consensus that sin does not destroy the human's image, but rather deforms and distorts it. Reformation thinkers approached the relation between sin and the *imago Dei* in such a way that they would be able to defend themselves against Arminian suppositions. In the Lutheran tradition the image is mainly understood in relation to original human righteousness (*iustitia originalis*). Sin is seen as having destroyed human image-bearing capabilities completely. Although both Luther and the Formula Concordiae speaks of the image in this manner, such a view is not used consistently within the Lutheran tradition.[34] Calvin distinguishes between humankind's natural gifts, which have been distorted, and their supernatural gifts, that have been taken away completely.[35] The natural gifts consist out of the will, mind and a capacity for discernment. These gifts have been ruined, but have not been completely destroyed, since they are part of the essence of human nature. There are still some shining sparks that indicate that humans differ from animals.[36] According to Calvin, the supernatural gifts consist of faith, love, justice and holiness. These gifts have been completely destroyed and can only be regained through regeneration.[37] When Calvin speaks of some remnants of the original *imago Dei* in human image-bearing, he does not deny the total depravity of the human. But for Calvin, total human depravity does not indicate that the human is dehumanised, or stops being human, but rather that all parts of a person's humanity is affected. Article 14 of the Belgic Confession and the Confessions of Dordt use the term *vestigia*. According to article 14 of the Belgic Confessions, remnants of a person's original gifts remain after the fall of the human. However, this *vestigia* does not relativise the total depravity

34. Cf. Berkouwer, *De mens het beeld Gods*, 43.
35. Cf. Calvin, *Institutio Christianae Religionis*, 2.2.12.
36. Ibid.
37. Ibid.

of the human, but actually intensifies the human situation of sin because it is an indication that there can be no absolution for the human. The Confessions of Dordt[38] speaks of a "light of nature" that remains in the person, but which is not enough for salvation. Clearly the Reformed Confessions do not use the concept of "remnants of goodness" to describe the human's sinful state as a partial corruption, but rather to indicate the full extent of the human's guilt and accountability before God.

Following in the footsteps of the Reformed Confessions, post Reformation Reformed theology often distinguished between the *imago Dei* in a broader and narrower sense.[39] In the broader sense the image denotes that sin does not dehumanise or demonise the human, but that God still maintains the sinful person as human. Yet the human loses the image quality in a narrower sense in that he or she lives estranged from God and forfeits the gifts of knowledge, justice and holiness.

The views of Barth, Thielicke and Brunner deserve particular mention because of their influence on twentieth century theology. Barth[40] is of the opinion that the image-bearing of the human does not point to a certain characteristic, but to humankind's ultimate destination. This means that the image cannot be lost, because what the human is destined for and does not yet possess, he can not loose. Naturally this does not mean that the image is merely a future promise, because the promise finds its fulfilment in Jesus Christ in Whom the first human was created.[41] The implication of Barth's view is that Christ does not become part of the human's nature, but the human rather becomes part of Christ's nature. The relationship between God and the human is thus based upon grace. The human was created for Christ.

Brunner[42] attempts to move away from the Reformational thought of a "remnant" of goodness in the human, the Catholic distinction between the human's natural and supernatural image and the radical view that the *humanum* has become a *profanum*. He distinguishes between the human's formal and material image. With these distinctions Brunner attempts to create a legitimate form of natural theology.[43] The

---

38. 3/4:4.

39. Berkouwer, *Die mens het beeld Gods*, 35.

40. Barth, *CD* III/2, 31.

41. Cf. Durand, *Skepping, mens en voorsienigheid*, 157.

42. Brunner, *Man in Revolt*, 95, 96.

43. Jónsson, *Image of God*, 70.

formal image indicates the human's form and structure, his *humanitas*, which he cannot loose.[44] The human still possesses his *ratio*, through which the Word of God can be received. However, a person's modus of existence changes from an existence in love to an existence under the law and judgement of God.[45] The material image, in contrast, indicates the characteristics of the human that have been lost through sin, but that can be granted again through the grace of God. The question, though, is whether Brunner's emphasis on the *ratio* of the human that forms the link between God and the human in spite of sin, adequately considers the total depravity of the human.

According to Thielicke[46] the human's image-bearing carries an indestructible character because the image denotes that God enters into a relationship with the human. Although human image-bearing possesses an ontic quality, the human is not defined by ontic characteristics. The image can not be distinguished from communion with God. Even after the Fall, the human still stands in a relationship with God, even if the relationship is negative in nature. The human lose the image only in the sense that a positive relationship with God is affected. However, this estrangement is rectified in Christ. The value of Thielicke's view lies therein that the human can not be abstracted from God. The question, though, is whether he does not allow the human's image-bearing to be absorbed in relational categories. Although human image-bearing contains a strong relational content, which indicates that the human being is determined by a relation with God, the *imago Dei* itself is not a relation, but has to do with the human in his totality.

The protological history in Genesis 1–11 clearly upholds the human's possession of the *imago Dei* even after the Fall. References to the human as being in image of God still appears in narratives after the fall of the human.[47] In Genesis 9 the commands of Genesis 1 are repeated and conveyed to humankind. Genesis 9:6 specifically mentions that there is something untouchable in the human, because neither human nor animal may take the life of a human. The New Testament nowhere describes the *imago Dei* as destroyed. On the contrary, in Jas 3:9 the

---

44. Brunner, *Man in Revolt*, 170.

45. Ibid., 103.

46. Thielicke, *Theological Ethics*, 159.

47. Gen 5:1b–2, 9:6.

image is brought into relation with the fact that the human was created by God and may therefore not be sworn at or treated hatefully.[48] The *perfectum* (*gegonatas*) is used to indicate that the human's likeness to God is still valid.

The fact that human image-bearing can not be destroyed by sin, does not mean that sin only affects the human partially. It rather means that God still preserves the human in spite of sin. Berkouwer[49] rightly states that a distinction should be made between human nature and sin. Sin lives in human nature, but it is not human nature itself. Even after the Fall humans remain an *opus et creatura Dei*. Precisely for this reason Christ can take on human nature. Sin deforms human image-bearing, but does not destroy the relationship with God, fellow human beings and the world. If the relational framework of human existence were destroyed, the human would cease to exist—if the human's image-bearing were totally ruined—he would not be entitled to dignity.

The Imago Dei in Christological Perspective

The Genesis version of the *imago Dei* offers a broad framework to understand the nature of the humankind's relationship with God, but at the same time gives the concept an open meaning which makes further theological reflection possible. A theological anthropology should therefore not be limited to a protological understanding of the *imago Dei*. The Christological foundation that the New Testament ascribes to the concept is of crucial importance for the further understanding of the concept, specifically with regard to the destination of the human.

The New Testament clearly contains an *imago Dei* Christology. In a certain sense the New Testamentical authors utilise the "open" meaning that the Priestly author ascribes to the image to further explicate the content thereof in the light of the coming of Jesus Christ. Jesus Christ is seen as the fulfilment of God's original purpose with the human. In Him the destination of the human's image-bearing becomes evident.

Some texts in the New Testament specifically refers to Jesus as the perfect image of God, while other texts apply the glory theology of the Old Testament to Christ. In 2 Cor 4:4 and 6, Christ is called the (*eikōn tou theou*) that emits the knowledge (*noemata*) and glory (*agnoesen*)

48. Cf. 1 Cor 11:7.

49. Berkouwer, *Die mens het beeld Gods*, 140.

of God. *Eikōn* is a Greek translation of *ṣelem*. It indicates a perfect reflection of an original prototype. Grenz[50] furthermore shows that *eikōn* indicates more than an image. The *eikōn* is also a participant of the reality which it reflects. 2 Corinthians 4 and 6, for example, states that Christ is more than a reflection of God. He is the Manifestation of God that emits the glory of God. God's being and character is reflected in a perfect manner in the life of Christ.

At the same time, Christ is the Example of the authentic human. Paul clearly uses the Priestly narrative's concept of the image-bearing nature of the human in 2 Corinthians 4 to indicate that Jesus is the Second Adam. Christ is the beginning of the new humanity, and at the same time the destination of the original humanity. He is the anti-type of Adam.[51] By relating Christ's image to his headship of the church, the *imago Dei* is placed within a social perspective in the sense that Christ's image-bearing has implications for the social structure of the new humanity.

In Col 1:15–20 Christ's image of God is used to give cosmological significance to Christ's rule. Christ is not only Redeemer in a soteriological sense, but He is the Creational Redeemer who rules from heaven over all history.[52] Colossians 1 thus expands and refines the theme of rule in Genesis 1. In Genesis 1 the human receives the mandate to rule over the creaturely, but Christ, who is the true image of God, receives the mandate to rule over the entire cosmos based on his reconciliatory work. Christ's rule emits the glory of God in a much more glorious way than do human beings. He is not merely image of God, He is the complete image of God.[53] Colossians 1:15 and 18 link Jesus's image specifically to the fact that He is the *protokos*—the first born of creation—and the first born from the dead. According to Macdonald[54] this term not only indicates the order of origin, but also the order of importance. The term is used to refer back to the original creation and to indicate the coming of a new creation. Christ was from the beginning, in a much more glorious sense than Adam, image of God as well as the first born

---

50. Grenz, "Jesus as the Imago Dei," 619.

51. Cf. Romans 5.

52. Cf. Standhartinger, *Studien zur Entstehungsgeschichte*, 206.

53. Macdonald, *Collosians, Ephesians*, 58.

54. Ibid.

of every creature. He is simultaneously the origin of the new creation that replaces the first creation of which Adam was the representative.

Apart from 2 Corinthians 4 and Colossians 1 that specifically refer to Christ as the perfect image of God, there are texts that, as already mentioned, apply the glory theology of the Old Testament to Christ. The status of glory that the Priestly creation narrative and other Old Testamentical texts such as Psalm 8 bestow on humanity as a whole, is conferred by these texts to the Person of Jesus, who is the representative of the new humanity. Hebrews 2:6–9 for instance quotes from Psalm 8 to indicate that it is the human's destination to rule over all things. This Old Testamentical promise is fulfilled in Jesus Christ to whom all things are subject, because of his vicarious suffering and death. In this manner the universal anthropology of Psalm 8 is made applicable to Christ. Hebrews 1:1–3 is a further example where Christ's image is directly related to his kingship. He is the equal of God who emits the glory of God. In His victory over sin and death He fulfils his role as Image of God and completes the calling of humanity. As a consequence he receives the right to rule over all things.

According to Smail[55] Christ's image of God entails that the *imago Dei* should be understood as a Trinitarian concept. Jesus Christus is the image of his Father and He manifests in the Holy Spirit. The human can only be a true image of God if he reflects the virtues of the relationship between the Father, Son and Holy Spirit in his life. Smail then continues to describe the *imago Dei* in the light of the perochetical relationship between the Father, Son and Holy Spirit. Human love ought to manifest something of the initiating love of God the Father, the responsive character of Christ's love and the revealing nature of the Holy Spirit's love. According to Smail the *Imago Dei* is synonomous with *Imago Trinitatis*.

The problem with a trinitarian approach is that the New Testament itself does not give a Trinitarian content to the *imago Dei*, but relates it exclusively to Christ. A Trinitarian approach creates endless posibilities for creative speculation. The precise relationship between the Triunity is essentially a mystery that defies human comprehension. The human can never embody the essence of God, in the same way as Christ does. There is, therefore, a certain discontinuity between the image of Christ and the image-bearing of the human. Although the human is able to

---

55. Smail, "In the Image of the Triune God," 27.

reflect God's virtues to some extent, there are virtues of God that the human can not reflect due to the radical dissimilarity between God and human beings.

The *Imago Dei* in Eschatological Perspective

The New Testament not only gives the *imago Dei* a Christological content, but also relates the concept to the creation of a new humanity with a specific divine destiny. Christ's coming is portrayed as an eschatological event. He reflects God's true purpose with the human. Because of Christ's work the Holy Spirit gradually repairs the human's original image so that it corresponds with the image of Christ. Although all people are called on to reflect the image of Christ in their lives, not all humans' images are recovered in Christ. The recovery of the image is an eschatological gift of God to his elected children. In Rom 8:29 and 30 Paul states that only those elected by the Father are destined to become like the image of his Son.[56] In these verses, the recovery of the image is specifically linked to God's election, the calling of the human, his redemption and sanctification. The theocentric foundation that the New Testament gives to the recovery of the *imago Dei* is of uttermost importance for a theological anthropology. The human is not an autonomous being that can salvage and sanctify the self. By self alone and in self the human cannot exist. The human can only reclaim true humanity if the relationship with God is repaired. So radical is human dependence on God, that a healing of the relationship with God cannot be effected through a person's private efforts. The initiative comes from God. This corresponds to the protological foundation that the Priestly narrative ascribes to the image: The human is a being focused on God, dependent on God, defined by his relationship with God, who finds his true destination in God.

In 2 Cor 3:18 the repairing of image-bearing is linked to the work of the Holy Spirit. The restoration of the image is an eschatological gift that starts in the present, but that is only fulfilled in the future. The central word in 2 Cor 3:18 is the passive verb (*metamorphoumetha*). It indicates an inner change in the human that is brought about by God so that the human can exhibit a new mode of being. Christ is the point of orientation and the end goal of the change, since the *metamorphou-*

56. Vorster, *Kerk en menseregte*, 326.

metha takes place in accordance with the image of Christ (*tēn autēn eikona*). The human is transformed to become like Christ not only to reflect Christ's virtues in his life, but also to stand in a relationship with God that is in accordance with God's will. All this is made possible by Christ.

The theological implication is that the eschatological destination of human becomes clear in the image of Christ. 2 Corinthians 3:18 states that the human is transformed from glory to glory (*apo doksēs eis doksan*) after the image of Christ. This does not mean that the human becomes divine or that some mystical unity between God and the human being exists, but rather that the human reflects the glory of Christ. The process of transformation to the image of Christ exhibits a continuity from one phase to another that shows increasing intensity and ultimately results in the *parousia*.[57]

In Eph 4:10 and Col 3:10 the content of the restored image is related to specific qualities. These qualities are divine gifts that enable the human to find the true destination. Colossians 3:10 relates the restored image to knowledge (*epignōsis*). It indicates an understanding of God's will that becomes visible in an intimate communion with God.[58] *Anakainomenon* qualifies the knowledge and indicates that an understanding of God's will can only be granted by God Himself. It can not be found by way of human reason. Ephesians 4:24 relates the human's image bearing to justice (*dikaiosunē*) and holiness (*osistēti*). Justice indicates a life in accordance with the will of God, while holiness designates an inner attitude in accordance with the will of God.[59] The above-mentioned Paulinic texts connect the restored image closely to the will of God. Knowledge is an understanding of God's will, justice is a life in agreement with God's will, and holiness is an inner attitude in accordance with God's will.

The establishment of a new humanity forms the climax of the salvation history and is the fulfilment of the *imago Dei* concept found in Genesis. The Adam-Christ typology that can be found in several Paulinic texts indicates that the creation of Adam does not encompass God's entire purpose with the human, but that God's purpose with the

---

57. Cf. Vorster, *Kerk en menseregte*, 326.

58. Cf. Louw and Nida, *Greek-English Lexicon of the New Testament*, 2:334.

59. Cf. ibid., 2:744–45.

human is only fully realised in the origin of the new humanity and their participation in the spiritual body of the Second Adam.[60]

The eschatological content that the New Testament gives to the human's image-bearing implies that human history is teleological in nature. According to Scripture the human history has a coherent form involving a Divine origin, a soteriological centre in the death and resurrection of Christ, and an eschatological end. Webster[61] rightly states that Scripture's emphasis on the teleological nature of human history should be distinguised from a "futurism" that aims at developing a coherent narrative scheme for human history through predictions of outcomes. The Christian eschatology does not have a technical character, but is inherently Christological. It has the Person of Christ as basis and content. Creation's history unfolds in a systematic way as a result of the change that Christ's coming has brought about. This teleological orientation of Christian eschatology presupposes that the human's existence can be purposeful, meaningful and hopeful. However, the Christian hope is not utopian in nature in the sense that the human can attain his or her own salvation, nor is it based on projections of outcomes, but it rather consists out of a faithful acceptance of God's promises that result in a moral-ethical life that transforms the world. The contradictions in history are ultimately not resolved within history, but on the level of the eternal and the Divine.[62]

Implications of the *Imago Dei* for Theological Anthropology

A theological anthropology can not merely be constructed based on the foundation of the *imago Dei*. Such an approach will be reductionist and will deny the rich diversity of anthropological perspectives in Scripture. Each locus in the Christian dogma, as well as other central themes in Scriptures such as the covenant, kingdom etc, is of importance for a theological anthropology. However, the following aspects of the *imago Dei* can in my view be utilised to construct a theological anthropology which might provide broad contours for the development of a Christian

60. Grenz, "Jesus as the Imago Dei," 623.

61. Webster, "Eschatology, Anthropology and Postmodernity," 21.

62. Cf. Niebuhr, *Nature and Destiny of Man*, 47.

anthropology. For the sake of conciseness a few concluding statements must suffice.

The Human Is a Religious Being

The human is a religious being created by God to live in the service of God. He is a transcendent being who's life is directed towards God, Who is the ground of the human's existence and who determines the destination of the human. God has created the human as a religious being who is dependent of Him, with the result that the human cannot escape religiosity. In the formation of a theological anthropology one should therefore first mention God before mentioning the human.[63] The direction of inquiry should proceed from theology to anthropology, and not the other way around, because the human can only be known in Christ, Who is the source of true knowledge of the human.

The Human Is a Free and Equal Being with Inherent Dignity

Because God creates the human after his image the human possesses an inherent dignity that animals do not enjoy. This status is not due to some extraordinary intrinsic abilities that the human possesses, but to God's grace, that grants him a special place in creation. Human dignity entails that humans have a right to realise the structural possibilities with which they were created. These structural possibilities comprise a right to life and security, to live in communion with God and fellow human beings, to work, practice culture and civilize God's creation according to the culture mandate.

Since God created all human beings after his image all human beings possess an equal worth and an inherent right to be treated as equals. This fundamental equality which is founded in the creative acts of God is realised in society when people are, as far as possible, given equal opportunities to realize their Godgiven structural possibilities in their personal, economic and social lives. A fundamental prerequisite for the attainment of social equality is that people should be treated justly and with love.

The relational nature of the *imago Dei* indicates that humans are created as free. Since freedom is a prerequisite for any authentic rela-

63. Durand, *Skepping, mens en voorsienigheid*, 139.

tionship, God created human beings with a free will. He did not create human beings as robots, but as beings who are able to make choices and to respond freely to him. Freedom is a reality made possible by God, a Divine gift, that exists therein that people are free to realize their structural possibilities and to find their Godgiven destiny.[64]

The Human Is a Sinful Being

The core of sin is when the human attempts to abstract himself from God. Sin affects all aspects of human existence. Humanity and sin are therefore inseparably linked to each other. A perfect analysis of human nature is impossible, because sin makes true self-knowledge impossible. Yet sin does not demonise or dehumanise the human. Sin is part of the human nature, but sin is not human nature. The human remains image of God despite sin, even though sin affects the human to such a degree, that from the very beginning, the full image of God cannot be exhibited. True humanity can only be found when the relationship between God and the human is fully restored.

The Human Is a Spiritual and Biological Being

According to the creation narratives the human is a spiritual being that receives his spirit from God (*nefesh*) and is therefore capable of leading a self-transcendent life. The human is at the same time a biological being that shares an environment with other creatures. The relationship between human and animal is, like the relationship between God and humankind, hierarchical in nature. The *imago Dei* indicates that the human has a higher status than animals. However, the human's right to rule over the creaturely sphere is not unlimited, but correlates with the duty to act responsibly towards the Creator. Humans may never destroy the community between the different creaturely spheres, but should conserve the delicate relationship between the different creaturely spheres in creation.

---

64. Section 2 of this book will focus in much more detail on the status of the human being as a free and equal being with inherent dignity.

The Human Is a Relational Being

The human is created to live in relationship with God, creation, his fellow man and himself. Due to the sinful nature of the human and the brokeness of his relations, the human cannot live separately from God and His redemptive actions. Only God can make possible the restoration of human relationships. Christ as the perfect Image of God is the point of orientation and example that should be followed in order to restore broken relationships.

The Human Is an Eschatological Being

Christian eschatology has two important implications for a theological anthropology. Firstly, the human is the object of God's grace. Central to human identity is the re-creative work of God that renews the human through the redemptive work of Christ and the sanctifying work of the Holy Spirit. Because of Christ's redemptive work, the human can find meaning in existence and need not be subjected to existential anxiety. Secondly, human existence is teleological in nature because the human's existence is connected with God's eschatological destination for Creation. This teleological understanding of human history stands in opposition to a postmodern view of history that views history as changing and discontinuous in nature.

2

Evil[1]

Introduction

THE REALITY OF EVIL IS ONE OF THE CHIEF INTELLECTUAL OBSTACLES in the Christian faith. It arises because of Christianity's insistence that God is an omnipotent being that is at the same time perfectly good. This creates the following logical problem: If God is an omnipotent being He must be able to destroy all evil, and if He is a perfectly good being he must want to abolish all evil. Yet evil exists. Therefore God must either not be omnipotent or not be perfectly good. The theological attempt to justify God's righteousness and goodness amidst the experience of moral and natural evil and suffering in the world is called theodicy (*theo-dike*). Though it can be argued that the human has no right to justify God and that sin is in its essence unintelligible, Christianity cannot avoid the question of the existence of evil, because it is a genuine difficulty.

This chapter analyses what John Hick calls in his famous book "Evil and the God of love" the "Augustinian type" of theodicy. This type of theodicy is characterised by an understanding of evil as defection and non-being, it shares a common belief in the original goodness of God's creation and that humans were created innocent, but exercised a good will badly, and it resists any doctrine of materialist dualism that posits the existence of a form of reality that is independent of God and stands in opposition to Him. John Hick suggests that the "Augustinian" type of theodicy is based on an outdated worldview derived from a literal-

---

1. This chapter was originally published as Nico Vorster, "The Augustinian Type of Theodicy: Is It Outdated?" *Journal of Reformed Theology* 5 (2011) 26–48. © 2011 Koninklijke Brill NV. Used by permission.

ist understanding of the creation narratives, and that it is impersonal and deterministic.[2] It therefore needs to be replaced with an "Irenaean" type of theodicy. This chapter examines his claim by asking whether the "Augustinian type" of theodicy is able to address the question of evil in a post-Newtonian world with an evolutionary understanding of reality. In order to answer the question the first section will critically evaluate the views of the three main theological exponents of the Augustinian type of theodicy on evil namely Augustine, John Calvin, and Karl Barth. The second section will identify apparent weaknesses in the Augustinian paradigm and attempt to assess whether these weaknesses can be addressed from within the Augustinian paradigm or whether the Augustinian paradigm, as Hick proposes, should be replaced altogether by another paradigm.

Augustine

Augustine struggled with the question of evil throughout his life. He debated the origin of evil as a Manichaean, and was still arguing it with Julian at the very end.[3] His doctrine on God resolutely affirms two basic premises: First, that God is an omnipotent being who is able to do whatever He wants insofar as such actions are consistent with His being, and secondly, that God is a good being and therefore not the direct cause of evil whatsoever. His doctrine on creation, accordingly, maintains that God created *ex nihilo* and therefore is sovereign over all things, and He created all things good because He is a good being.

Augustine formulated his views on evil against the background of his struggle with Manichaeanism. The Manichaeans described evil as an ontological force that stems from matter, opposes the divine, and compels the innately good souls of human beings to sin.[4] They thereby eliminated the moral dimension of evil and the personal accountability of the human being. Augustine adopted and modified the notion of evil as privation from Neo-Platonism to emphasize that evil is not a cosmic ontological principle that opposes goodness. In his view, evil is not a substance in itself, but is rather a form of defection, the absence

2. Cf. Hick, *Evil and the God of Love*, 193–200.

3. Rist, *Augustine*, 261.

4. Bonner, *St Augustine of Hippo*, 317. Babcock, "Augustine on Sin and Moral Agency," 31.

of good and the corruption of being. It is committed by moral agents who are responsible for their own actions. God is therefore not unjust when he holds humanity accountable for their sins. Yet, even though humans are capable of moral evil, they were created good by God. God is in no way the source of evil or the Creator of human sin.[5] Augustine was able to reconcile his position on human accountability for sin with his view that God is not the source of evil by employing the concept of the free will of man. It provided him with a mechanism through which something that came forth from God as good, could at the same time be capable of evil.[6] Augustine regarded the human will as a spiritual good that is necessary for living rightly, but capable of being used wrongly. A genuine free will necessarily carries with it the liability to sin. But without having freedom of choice, with its built-in liability, humans would lack the capacity to choose to live rightly.[7]

However, after 392 Augustine began to modify his original position regarding the free will as something that all human beings possess. In his polemic against Fortunatus he shifted the free exercise of will from all human beings to only the first human being, thereby abandoning a crucial element in his earlier argument for human agency in moral evil.[8] As a consequence of the first man's voluntary sin the whole of humankind descended into the necessity of habit and bondage to sin and death. The human's compulsion to sin is thus caused by an initial sin. After the first sin, all humans sin involuntarily. Nonetheless, these actions can still be interpreted as the agents' own.[9]

Augustine developed his argument on the nature of the human's free will and original sin further in his polemic writings against the Pelagians. The Pelagians held that the human's natural faculties are created good. Humankind can therefore be without sin if it chose to be. Though humankind's mind is clouded by sin, it can be illuminated again by the Law and the Gospel. Augustine, however, insisted that the Fall of Humankind led to a total disintegration of human nature, a shift

---

5. Augustine, "De Civitate Dei," Book XII.

6. Cf. Babcock, "Augustine on Sin and Moral Agency," 33.

7. Mann, "Augustine on Evil and Original Sin," 46.

8. Augustine, "Acta seu Disputatio," XXII; Babcock, "Augustine on Sin and Moral Agency," 40.

9. Augustine, "Acta seu Disputatio," XXII; Babcock, "Augustine on Sin and Moral Agency," 38.

in the orientation of the will, that is, a turn from a higher state of being to a lower state of being, from God to the self, thereby making itself rather than God the principle of its existence.[10]

In *De Natura et Gratia*[11] he states that the human originally had a free will, but that original sin darkened and flawed the human's will so that human nature itself is corrupted. Not only did the Fall lead to moral evil, but also natural evil. The Fall weakened all of man's faculties so that he becomes liable to disease, impotent to rule the desires of the body and subject to death.[12] Sin is therefore not something external to humankind. It is in us, part of our nature. However, this "naturalness" is a false naturalness that is parasitic on a deeper good nature.[13]

Augustine thus combined the concepts of the free will of man and original sin in order to preserve God's ultimate power and infinite goodness, but to stress at the same time that the nothingness of privation is a power superior to any individual will or singular volition. The problem that Augustine still had to face was: How did the first evil act arise?

Augustine' answer is that the evil will is uncaused, in contrast to good will that is specifically affected by God. Evil willing is a self-originating act and therefore not explicable in terms of causes. In *De Civitate Dei* Augustine states that evil is not a matter of efficiency but of deficiency. Trying to discover the causes of defection is like trying to see darkness or hear silence. As darkness is the absence of light and silence the absence of sound, deficient causality is the absence of cause. The cause of evil is rather the defection of the will of a being that is mutably good from the Good that is immutable. This happened first in

---

10. Augustine, "De Civitate Dei," Book XIV.13.

11. Augustine, "De Natura et Gratia," III:
    Natura quipped hominis primitus inculpate et sine ullo vitio create est, naturo vero ista hominis, qua unusquisque ex Adam nascitur, jam medico indigent, qui sana non est. Omnia quidem bona, quae habet informatione, vita sensibus, mente a summon Deo habet creatore et artifice suo. Vitium vero, quod ista naturalia bona contenebrat et infirmat, ut illuminatione et curatione opus habeat, non ab inculpabili artifice contractum est, sed ex originali peccato, quod commisum est libero arbitrio.

12. Augustine, "De Perfectione Justitiae Hominis," II.

13. Cf. Mathewes, *Evil and the Augustinian Tradition*, 74.

the case of the angels, and afterwards in the human being.[14] By not only understanding sin anthropologically as an original perversion, but also ontologically as a primordial perversion, Augustine emphasizes that evil is totally alien to God's created order. Evil is a corruption of good and can only be as long as there is something good to be corrupted. By definition it cannot exist on its own. Augustine's description of evil as a lack of being invests God with perfect goodness. If evil is the lack of being, then God cannot have willed evil, because God's will is precisely what is not evil. It is also a corollary of His emphasis on God's infinite power. Evil can because of its secondary nature never overpower God's natural order.

Augustine thus understands evil as non-being. Central to the notion of evil as non-being is the understanding of evil as a kind of nothingness that had fallen away from being. Since "nothing" has no substance of its own, it is impossible to define except over and against "being."

Though Augustine views the introduction of evil into a wholly good creation as fundamentally an incomprehensibly negative act, it does not fall outside of God's providence. In his doctrine on predestination Augustine states that God foresaw the human's fall before the creation of the world and planned its compatibility with the balanced perfection of the universe.[15] This allows him to soften the underlying contradictions between God's omnipotence and goodness. Though God does not will evil, it is still part of His providence in that it falls under His jurisdiction and has an instrumental value for God: God brings good from evil, the existence of evil contributes to the beauty of the whole, evil serves as a warning against hidden pride . . .[16]

Augustine's attempt to demythologise the Manichaean view of evil deserves praise. He profoundly challenged a materialist worldview that saw the cosmos as the battlefield of the eternal forces of good and evil. His doctrine on evil contain the basic premises for an authentic Christian approach to evil, namely that God is sovereign, that he created *ex nihilo*, that evil was not created by God, that God is goodness and that the human is complicit to injustice and suffering. He also over-

14. Augustine, "De Civitate Dei," XII.9; Hick, *Evil and the God of Love*, 59.

15. Cf. Hick, *Evil and the God of Love*, 69.

16. Cf. Augustine, "De Civitate Dei," XI.17; XI.23.

comes the Platonic, Neo-Platonic, Gnostic and Manichaean prejudices against matter and lays the foundation for a Christian naturalism that rejoices in the world.[17]

The most problematic aspect in Augustine's teaching is his notion that evil is fundamentally a perversion of good that exists parasitically on the good. He essentially distinguishes between two human natures. The first nature is wholly good, while the second is a perversion of the first. Augustine derives this notion from a literal understanding of the creation narratives: God created all things in a good state. Then came a Fall that perverted the original good nature of creation and introduced evil, which exists parasitically on the original good nature. However this notion is outdated in the light of the evidence of biological history. There was no initial wholly good nature that was perverted, nature always contained a dark side. Suffering, predation, death and pain were there before the arrival of the human. A further question is whether Augustine does not diminish the power and terror of evil by describing evil as deficiency, corruption, a lack of good and as negative and privative. Is evil not more than a mere absence of good, a passive defection? Does such a definition of evil do justice to the horror that evil causes? Most victims do not experience evil as mere absence, but as a brutal, direct and malevolent force. Evil is not merely a refusal to act or an attempt to try to be independent of God that ends up in a perverted parody, but it often amounts to full resistance and revolt against God and humanity.

John Calvin

Calvin did not develop a theodicy in the technical sense and would probably object to the question on theodicy as posed by Leibniz and other philosophers. For Calvin the origin of sin and the relation of sin to God's will is a mystery. Not surprisingly, Berkhof criticises Calvin for taking refuge in incomprehensibility.[18] But Calvin's approach to the mystery of evil corresponds with one of the most important premises in his theology, namely that to know God is in essence too high for us. His majesty is hidden and remote from our sense.[19] The human,

17. Hick, *Evil and the God of Love*, 45.

18. Berkhof, *Christian Faith*, 221.

19. Calvin, *Inst.*, 1.5.1.

therefore, has no right to search for illicit knowledge that falls outside God's revelation.[20] It is precisely man's urge for illicit knowledge that caused the Fall. To seek illicit knowledge is to commit an act of vanity that denies the otherness of God and the radical distinction between God and humans. Instead, we ought to be content to accept that human reason has its limits and to trust that all God's acts are good and wise.

Calvin maintains that all things, even the most minor events in life, are subject to God's will.[21] What appears to us externally as mere contingency or serendipity, faith recognises as nothing else than the hidden impulse of providence.[22] In his commentary on Job, Calvin distinguishes between God's guidance in the realm of nature and history. In both realms, God directly controls and wills every event. He does not simply permit earthly occurrences, but commands the entire course of nature and history. God's providence is not merely general in nature, but He is deeply involved in the particulars of history.[23] Even Satan can do nothing without the permission of God. The metaphor that Calvin often employs is that God "bridles" Satan so that nothing is outside of his control.[24] This seemingly deterministic view of God's providence is closely connected to his understanding of God's eternal predestination. Calvin understands the predestination to be an eternal pre-creational decision of God in which He determined what He wills for every person's life. God's eternal decision is not based on some foreknowledge as if humans could contribute to their own salvation through their virtues, but it rests solely on his will.[25] The elect do not differ from all others except that they are protected by God's special mercy from rushing into the final ruin of death.[26] In His damnation of some God exhibits his anger over sin and His condemnation thereof. God, after all, has the right to bestow his grace on some and deny his grace for others.[27]

Though Calvin often employs the term permission, especially in his sermons, he is critical of the idea that God does not will sin, but

---

20. Calvin, *Genesis*, 1:153.

21. Calvin, *Inst.*, 1.16.2.

22. Ibid., 1.16.9. Cf. Kirby, "Stoic and Epicurean?," 317.

23. Schreiner, "Through a Mirror Dimly," 180. Cf. Calvin, *Inst.*, 1.16.8.

24. Schreiner, "Calvin's Sermons," 181; *Inst.*, 1.16.3.

25. Calvin, *Inst.*, 3.22.3.

26. Ibid., 3.14.10.

27. Ibid., 3.22.6.

permits sin, because such a distinction limits God's sovereignty and weakens the witness of Scripture. It creates the impression that God is a spectator who creates the possibility of sin and waits to see whether humankind will use their freedom to sin or not.[28] Calvin is adamant that we may never use the concept of permission to nullify God's providence.[29] God's permission is part of God's active will. His permission is not a general permission, but a willing permission of every particular evil. Whatever we conceive of in our own minds is directed to its own end by God's secret inspiration.[30] According to Calvin, God not only foresaw the Fall, but He compelled it.[31] After all, He could have prevented it, had He seen fit to do so.[32] In his commentary on Genesis 3 Calvin states:

> When I say, however, that Adam did not fall without the ordination and will of God, I do not take it as if sin had ever been pleasing to Him, or as if he simply wished that the precept which he had given should be violated So far as the fall of Adam was the subversion of equity, and of well constituted order, so far as it was contumacy against the Divine-Law giver, and the transgression of righteousness, certainly it was against the will of God; yet none of these things render it impossible that in a certain sense, although to us unknown He might will the fall.[33]

Thus, though we cannot comprehend the reason for God's acts, we must be satisfied to accept the testimony of Scripture that God wills sin. That God has a definite goal for sin and uses it to reach His destination, becomes clear in the cross of Christ in which the guilt of humankind and the love and righteousness of God is revealed.[34]

Even though God wills sin, Calvin states categorically that humankind may never blame God for its sins.[35] Sin does not occur outside of the human's will, it is no external coercive force that engulfs humankind, but it is inherently part of human nature and finds its roots in

28. Ibid., 1.18.1, 3. 23.8.
29. Ibid., 1.18.2.
30. Ibid.
31. Ibid., 3.23.8.
32. Calvin, *Genesis*, 144.
33. Ibid.
34. Calvin, *Inst.* 1.18.4.
35. Ibid., 1.17.5.

the lusts of man.[36] Man was created flexible and sinned voluntarily and therefore bears the quilt for sin.[37] The question is: How can God will sin or use sin without being the author of sin or being stained by sin? In his commentary on Genesis 3 Calvin employs the Augustinian notion of defection:

> It is an impious madness to ascribe to God the creation of any evil and corrupt nature; for when he completed the world, he himself gave this testimony to all his works, that they were "very good." Wherefore, without controversy, we must conclude, that the principle of evil with which Satan was endued was not from nature, but from defection; because he had departed from God, the fountain of justice and all rectitude.[38]

Later on he also attributes the fall of Adam and Eve to defection.[39] Clearly Calvin is of the opinion that God neither created man nor nature sinful or evil, but that the human acted according to his own will. Yet, God did not prevent the Fall, but allowed and permitted it to serve his good purposes.[40] God's permission of sin does not stain God because His motive is righteous and serve the good. The metaphor that Calvin uses in this regard is that the sun's rays make a corpse stink, but do not stink themselves.[41] Kirby rightly notes that central to Calvin's argument is an adherence to a due distinction between "instrument" and "end." Calvin is able to see human sinfulness itself as an instrument of divine providence while denying, on the ground of the self same distinction that his instrumentality provides any excuse whosoever for human misdeeds. Even if man sins from necessity he still remains a free and responsible agent, for he is acting voluntarily and not from external compulsion.[42] In any case, man has no right to ask God to justify himself to humankind or to give any reasons for His acts.[43] In fact, God's will is the highest measure of righteousness. We must consider

36. Ibid., 3.5.5, 3.23.9.

37. Calvin, *Genesis*, 158.

38. Ibid., 142.

39. Ibid., 152.

40. Calvin, *Inst.* 1.17.5.

41. Ibid.

42. Cf. ibid., 2.4.1.

43. Ibid., 3.23.5.

everything that God wills as righteous simply because He wills it. When we are asked why God wills something, our reply simply ought to be: because He wills it.[44]

Calvin not only grounds the fall of Adam in the will of God, but also the results of the Fall on the human race and nature. With regard to the human race he states:

> For the human race has not naturally derived corruption through its descent from Adam, but that result is rather to be traced to the appointment of God.[45]

With regard to nature he then states:

> The Lord, however, determined that his anger should, like a deluge, overflow all parts of the earth, that wherever man might look, the atrocity of sin should meet his eyes. Before the Fall, the state of the world was a most fair and delightful mirror of the divine favour and paternal indulgences towards man. Now in all the elements we perceive that we are cursed.

For Calvin moral and natural evil proceed from the same fountain.[46] God requires that both his mercy and grace and His wrath and justice are displayed in his creatures. The corruption of both human nature and nature itself is according to Calvin an expression of God's anger and serves to punish the damned and chastise the believers.[47] Yet, in his sermons on Job, he also states that we must be cautious not to think that we can understand the justice of God. Fallen and redeemed wisdom both suffer the noetic effect of sin and stand far removed from the inscrutable and secret justice of God. History does not clearly reflect God's wisdom. We, therefore, can only find solace in the unchangeable attributes of God.[48]

Though Calvin's doctrines on providence and predestination might seem harsh, he clearly had therapeutic intentions with these doctrines. He attempted to break with the commonly held Epicurean belief that history is dictated by chance. Instead the believer can find his solace in God's will and providence that remind us that everything

44. Ibid., 3.23.2.

45. Calvin, *Genesis*, 156.

46. Cf. ibid., 177.

47. Cf. Calvin, *Inst.*, 1.17.1.

48. Cf. Schreiner, "Calvin's Sermons," 183–86.

that happens, whether good or bad, has a purpose and eventually serve God's good intentions. Yet his treatment of the subject is generally characterised by ambiguity, a continuous tension between the revealed and the not revealed, and paradoxes. He reaches an almost intolerable paradox when he states that God wills sin and permits evil but that God is not the author of sin or evil. The question is: Is such a notion really coherent? Can one who uses sin as an instrument really be acquitted from the stain of sin simply because he uses it for a good end? Would a good God ever use sin as an instrument? Calvin's direct ascription of evil to the will of God also creates other questions regarding God's goodness: Would a good God allow sin so that he can show his anger to the damned? If God "bridles" evil so that it cannot commit more evil than God allows, why would a loving God allow so much brutal, senseless and malevolent evil in the world? Calvin is so set on stressing God's omnipotence that He brings into question God's goodness and holiness. The Heidelberg Catechism, Gallic Confession and Belgic Confession do not follow Calvin's strict logic, but the infra-lapsarian line according to which God in just punishment leaves people because of their sin in the perdition to which they condemned themselves.[49]

Karl Barth

The reality of evil is for Barth a clear demonstration of the brokenness of all theological thought. It is broken in the sense that it can progress only in isolated thoughts and statements directed from different angles. We can never seize the object of evil or create a comprehensive system that explains evil.[50]

Barth's approach to evil can be characterised as Christocentric. God created in order that Jesus Christ shall exist. He defines creation as the external basis of the covenant and the covenant as the inner basis of creation.[51] Creation provides the sphere in which the institution of the covenant takes place, while the covenant is the goal of all God's works. The remark in Gen 1:31 that the creation was created good, is not a description of the cosmos as such, but must be seen in relation to Christ. The creation is good because it finds its goal and true mean-

49. Berkhof, *Christian Faith*, 485.
50. Barth, *KD* III/3, 332.
51. Ibid., 103.

ing in Christ and the covenant.[52] Because of Christ the created world is already perfect, despite its imperfection.[53]

As is the case with Augustine, Barth utilises the concept of the free will of man to explain the origin of evil. God created the creation free. It therefore had the possibility of self-annulment and its own destruction. Without the possibility of defection or evil, creation would not be distinct from God and therefore not be His creation. A creature freed from the possibility of falling away would not really be living as a creature.[54]

Sin is when the creature opposes God and the meaning of its own existence by rejecting God's preserving grace. The fault is that of the creature and not of God or the nature of creation. The fact of evil does not cast any shadow on God because it does not find its origin either in God Himself or in His being and activity as the Creator.[55] God opposes the defection and destruction of the creature because He cannot cease to be God or cease to act as the Creator and Lord of the world, and therefore of the sinful world. His reply is rather to justify and maintain Himself in relation to the sinful world by resisting and overcoming sin.[56]

According to Barth evil, sin, wickedness, the devil, death and non-being exists in its own way by the will of God.[57] Nothing exists outside of the will of God. He distinguishes between God's *voluntas efficiens* and *voluntas permittens* to explain the way in which evil exists by the sovereign will of God. God's *voluntas efficiens* is that what God positively affirms and creates, while His *voluntas permittens* consists in His refraining, non-prevention and non-exclusion. God not only gives the creature its existence and being, freedom and independence (*voluntas efficere*), but also refrains from making it impossible for man to misuse its independence and freedom (*voluntas permittens*). God creates in such a way that He also permits. The *voluntas permittens* is no less

---

52. Barth, *KD* III/I, 380.

53. Ibid., 389.

54. Barth, *KD* II/1, 566:
    Ohne die so verstandene Möglichkeit des Abfalls oder des Bösen würde die Schöpfung von Gott nich verschieden und also als seine Schöpfung nich wirklich sein. Es bedeutet also keine Unvollkommenheit der Schöpfung und des Schöpfers, dass des Geschöpf von ihm abfallen und verloren gehen kann.

55. Ibid., 566.

56. Ibid., 566–67.

57. Ibid., 670.

volunta divina than the *voluntas efficiens*, yet it is only a permission, a restricted toleration.[58] The question is: Why is God's will for creation not only a *voluntas efficiens*, a good will? Barth's precarious answer is that creation has to be constantly reminded of God's grace. God's grace depends on the existence of a divine *voluntas permittens*, and in virtue of this on the reality of disgrace, damnation and hell.[59] Barth does not see good and evil as two separate poles alongside each other, but he sees the whole of creation from the perspective of Christ. Since everything is created for Jesus Christ and his death and resurrection, everything from the very outset must stand under this twofold and contradictory determination.

Barth calls the reality that opposes and resists God's world dominion *das Nichtige*.[60] *Das Nichtige* is some kind of third factor that can neither be explained from the side of the Creator nor the creature, but can only be regarded as hostility to both. It must not be identified with the negative shadow side of creation that is the result of the creation's creatureliness, and is actually part of God's good intent. Rather it is that which is an insult to the Creator and that contradicts God's self manifestation in Jesus Christ.[61] The true nature of *das Nichtige* is revealed in Jesus Christ, because in Jesus Christ is not only revealed what is good, but also what is utterly distinct from God. The coming of Christ is a sign that God takes the challenge to Him and his Creation to heart.[62] *Das Nichtige* is thus the reality that opposes and resists God and is utterly distinct from Him. It is that which brought Jesus Christ to the cross and that which he defeated there. It is not nothing, but exists in its own curious fashion, it is in no way an attribute of God or the creaturely being, we know it only through God's self-revelation, it is grounded in God's not willing and it is evil in nature.[63] The concrete form in which *das Nichtige* is active is the sin of humanity, because in sin it becomes man's own act, achievement and guilt. Sin, after all, consists therein that the human repudiates God's grace and command.

58. Ibid., 671.
59. Ibid.
60. Barth, *KD* III/3, 327.
61. Ibid., 334–42.
62. Ibid., 341.
63. Ibid., 416.

Yet *das Nichtige* is not exhausted in sin. It is also something under which we suffer in connection with sin. Sin is attended and followed by the suffering of evil and death, which in itself only belongs to the shadow side of creation, but which now becomes intolerable life destroying things. That *das Nichtige* has the form of evil and death as well as sin shows that it is not only moral in nature, but also physical and total. As such it is superior to all the forces that humankind can assemble against it. Evil and death may be distinguished from sin in that evil primarily attack the creature and indirectly God, while sin attacks God directly.[64] *Das Nichtige* is real as such because it, too, owes its existence to God in the sense that it is that which he has not elected and not willed, but ignored, rejected, excluded and judged. It is a reality that was not created but posited, a reality that while it has no basis in itself it lives through it's antithesis to God's grace.[65] In this sense *das Nichtige* is really privation, the attempt to defraud God of his honour and right and at the same time to rob the creature of its salvation and right.[66] Because *das Nichtige* has no autonomous existence of its own, it cannot possess unlimited power. It exists only through God, in the power of divine negation and rejection.[67] The conquest, removal and abolition of *das Nichtige* are entirely God's own affair. Only He can master *das Nichtige* and guide the course of history towards this victory.[68] *Das Nichtige* therefore has a paradoxical status: It is utterly inimical to God, yet God controls it.

Karl Barth makes an important contribution to the debate on theodicy by approaching the problem from the perspective of Christ. Since Christ is God's solution to suffering, any Christian debate on theodicy should start with Christ and the cross. Only in Christ a positive theodicy is possible. A natural approach to theodicy that takes its premise in human experience can not transcend the negative dimension of evil. Barth also makes considerable effort to depict evil as something that is irreconcilable with the will of God, something that can only be the object of fear and loathing. His distinction between the shadow side of creation that are due to creaturely limitedness and evil that is enmity

64. Ibid., 342–55.

65. Ibid., 375, 376.

66. Ibid., 408.

67. Ibid., 381.

68. Ibid., 409.

against God is a particular helpful construction that brings some clarity on the subject. However, there are many tensions inherent in Barth's approach to evil.

John Hick rightly criticizes Barth's notion that by willing a good creation God unwilled its opposite, which is *das Nichtige*. This view is rather speculative in nature and contradicts Barth's own resistance to speculative theorizing. By using this concept he goes beyond the data of faith and becomes entangled in the dangers of philosophical construction.[69] Furthermore, it makes no rational sense to attribute the existence of *das Nichtige* to God's not-willing. Does that mean that God unwillingly brings forth evil through His creative acts?

Barth's treatment of the nature of God's will seems to be full of contradictions. In his doctrine on creation he ascribes the existence of *das Nichtige* to God's not willing. Yet in his doctrine on God he speaks with regard to the existence of evil of God's permissive will that entails that God permits evil in order that Christ should exist. The latter notion is problematic because it implies that God willed evil (even if just in a permissive way) so that He can show us grace. This raises a serious question: is God's grace dependent on evil? Apart from the fact that this hypothesis endangers the moral perfectness of God Scripture does not speak of God's grace in this way. God's grace is not presented in Scripture in objectivist categories, but is seen as God's answer to suffering and evil.

Weaknesses and Strengths in the Augustinian Type of Theodicy

The Inevitability of Sin and the Accountability of the Human

The "Augustinian" type of theodicy contains an inherent tension between the all-encompassing will of God, the inevitability of sin and the accountability of the human being. Calvin's theology reaches a total impasse in this regard because of his supra-lapsarian grounding of sin in God's will.[70] His notion that a sinner sins necessarily because God wills sin, but that man is still responsible for its own sin is not tenable. Barth

---

69. Hick, *Evil and the God of Love*, 135–36.

70. It must be noted that Calvin is not consistently supra-lapsarian in his view of the ordering of divine decrees.

attempts to solve the impasse by describing the election as solely and totally grace in Christ. God damns and elects all humanity in Christ. Humanity thus participates in the election of Christ. The question is whether Barth's view on election takes humankind's accountability for sin seriously. His doctrine on election, furthermore, leads to a doctrine of universal reconciliation that is not in accordance with Scripture.

The solution to this inherent problem in the "Augustinian" type of theodicy might exist in the concept of the original free will of the human that both Augustine and Barth employ, but do not bring to its full conclusion. The notion of God's permission would indeed be problematic, as Calvin suggests, if it is used in the sense that there is a synergy between the work of God and man, but not if it is understood as expressing the way in which God grants man creaturely freedom within His reign. Creaturely freedom does not endanger or limit the sovereign and omnipotent acts of God.[71] Since goodness and love are characteristics of God's being He recognises true freedom, because communication of love can only take place in freedom. God's love entails that He creates in a free decision a world that is independent of Him, thereby limiting Himself and providing space for creaturely freedom. If we do not allow for creaturely freedom we also leave no room for human responsibility and accountability.

Alvin Plantinga made an important contribution to the theodicy debate through his explication of a systematic free-will defence. He does not offer the free-will defence as a theodicy, but as a "defence" in the face of a purely logical challenge. The premise of the free-will defence is that God wanted man to love him spontaneously and not because of coercion. God chose for a free creation that is independent of Him. This logically entails that the human being has the potential to defect. Without the possibility of defection, creation would not be distinct from God and therefore not be His creation. Plantinga's argument is that a world containing creatures that are significantly free is more valuable than a world containing no free creatures at all. God can create free creatures, but he cannot cause or determine them to do what is only right, for if he does so they are not significantly free. In order to create creatures capable of moral good, therefore, he must create creatures capable of moral evil. He cannot leave these creatures free to perform

---

71. Cf. Berkouwer, *De voorzienigheid Gods*, 167.

evil and at the same time prevent them from doing so.[72] According to Plantinga God did in fact create significantly free creatures, but some of them went wrong in the exercise of their freedom. This is the source of moral evil. The fact that these creatures sometimes go wrong, however, neither counts against God's omnipotence nor against His goodness, for He could have forestalled the occurrence of moral evil only by excising the possibility of moral good.[73] In other words, it is possible that God cannot bring forth a good state of affairs without permitting evil.

If we follow Plantinga's free-will defence we can state that God is neither the author of sin nor wills sin, but that sin is the result of the free actions of human beings.

The Fall

The rise of an evolutionary worldview due to discoveries in biology, palaeontology and physics, complicates the question of evil to a degree that neither Augustine, nor Calvin or Barth could foresee. Due to discoveries in the natural sciences we know today that the conditions that cause human disease and mortality were already part of the natural order before the emergence of man.[74]

The traditional answer of the "Augustinian" type of theodicy that there was once a wholly good creation in which man enjoyed a serene consciousness of God, but that this good world became distorted after the fall of Adam and that the whole of humanity inherited their guilt and a corrupted and sin-prone nature, because they stand in a corporate unity and continuity of life with the primal pair, seems to be insufficient to face the challenge of evolution theory.

As noted earlier, John Hick, suggests that the "Augustinian" type of theodicy ought to be replaced by an "Irenaean" type of theodicy. According to the "Irenaean" view the human's basic nature in distinction from animals is that of a personal being endowed with moral freedom and responsibility. However, the human is not as yet the perfected being that God seeks to produce, he is an imperfect and immature being at the beginning of a process of growth and development in God's continuing providence, which will culminate in the finite "likeness" of

72. Plantinga, *Nature of Necessity*, 166–67.

73. Ibid.

74. Hick, *Evil and the God of Love*, 201, 249.

God.[75] The original human being is only the raw material for a further and more difficult stage in God's creative work. Hick combines this view with evolutionary theory. The creation of the human has two stages, namely his fashioning as *homo sapiens* through the evolutionary process, and his spiritualisation as child of God. Humans can, however, not be perfected through divine fiat, but only through the uncompelled responses and willing co-operation of individuals, through a hazardous adventure in individual freedom.[76] If a person has to develop, this world must become a place of soul-making.

Why can't God create human beings that freely do what is right? Hick's answer is that there is no point in the creation of finite persons unless they could be endowed with a degree of genuine freedom and independence over against their Maker. This does not mean that God affords the human random and undetermined freedom, but He provides the human with limited creativity and autonomy so that his character is partially formed and partially re-formed in the very moment of decision.[77] In causing man to evolve in this way out of lower forms of life, God has placed His human creature away from the immediate divine presence in a world with its own structure and laws in which he has a relative but real autonomy and freedom over and against his Creator. The human did not fall into this state of being from a prior state of holiness, but was brought into being in this way as a creature capable of eventually attaining holiness.[78]

For the world to be a place of soul-making it should contain real hardships and challenges. All the unjust and apparently wasted suffering in the world may be regarded as a divinely created sphere of soul-making.[79] Even animal pain is justified if it plays its part in indirectly forming the human as a child of God.[80] Yet, such suffering only receives meaning in the creature's joyous participation in the completed creation. In faith we must affirm that there will be no personal life that is unperfected and no suffering that will not eventually become a phase

75. Ibid., 212.

76. Ibid., 255.

77. Ibid., 275–77.

78. Ibid., 286–87.

79. Ibid., 336.

80. Ibid., 316.

in the fulfilment of God's good purpose.[81] Hick's position thus has two major premises: Firstly, evil is a necessary element in our maturation, secondly, that it is finally converted into goodness by the grace of God. He grounds evil in the will of God in order to maintain these two positions.

Ironically Hick's theodicy is not free of the same inconsistencies that he identifies in the "Augustinian" type of theodicy. By locating evil in the will of God, Hick risks setting God the Redeemer against God the Creator. On the one hand God creates through evolution and the use of suffering, yet on the other God identifies with the suffering through a fellow-suffering. It is difficult to understand why Hick gives instrumental value to something that Scripture describes as contrary and alien to the will of God, as something that stands under God's no. Is all the evil that God supposedly allows on earth, really there only for the purpose of soul-making? Would a good God allow so much suffering only for the purpose of creating mature human beings? Is the means that God supposedly use to serve His ends, the means that a good God would use? Hick has rightly been criticized for the purposive quality that he attributes to evil. Meslé, for instance, accuses Hick of actually denying the reality of evil. According to Meslé, we must abandon any false comfort that bad things are really good or that evil will ultimately and inevitably be turned into good. Some suffering is truly evil and irredeemable.[82] Geivett's[83] main critique against Hick is that it would be immoral of God to cause evil and to use evil in order to create good souls. We may also ask whether Hick's notion that God sets Himself in an epistemic distance from humans and then uses evil to make a person enter into a relationship with him does not amount to a form of coercion? Furthermore, why would virtues earned through a process of soul making be better than virtues bestowed by God as an innate element of personhood?

The "Augustinian" type of theodicy is more sound than the "Ireneaen" type because it attempts not to attribute evil to God. It stays true to the Scriptural motives on creation, it takes the biblical notions of a Fall and election seriously, and it emphasizes the accountability

81. Ibid., 340.
82. Meslé, *John Hick's Theodicy*, 19.
83. Geivett, *Evil and the Evidence of God*.

of the human being for sin. Karl Barth, furthermore, has shown that an "Augustinian" type of theodicy is not necessarily dependent on a strictly literalist interpretation of the creation narratives. I therefore would suggest an alternative solution that stays true to the witness of Scripture and preserve the strengths in the "Augustinian" theodicy. This is to be found, firstly, in an understanding of the Fall as an event in time but with eternal significance, and, secondly, in relating the concept of *creatio continua* to God's providence.

The notion of a Fall is increasingly rejected in theological circles, because of the already mentioned developments in natural sciences. However, if we reject the notion of a Fall we can come to no other conclusion namely that God is either the author of sin or that evil is an independent ontological reality. This is the weakness in Hick's theodicy. Understanding the Fall as an event in time with eternal significance might solve the impasse. It entails that time cannot be understood in linear terms. Theologically speaking the problem with a linear concept of time is that eternity is dissolved into time. Relativity theory in theoretical physics, furthermore, has shown that the linear concept of time that pervaded seventeenth-century mechanistic science is deficient. It states that there is an a-temporal spacetime continuum, because the metrical structure of space and time cannot be abstracted from the presence of physical objects, rather physical objects are accounted for as effects of the gravitational field of spacetime.[84] There is thus an interdependence between physical objects and the spatial and temporal dimensions of their existence. This notion of space time is closely connected to the "block universe" theory. According to this theory time has an objective quality because—seen from a particular point of reference—time does not change. Past, present and future all exist simultaneously. Russel Stannard,[85] therefore, distinguishes between objective time as seen from the perspective of theoretical physics, and subjective time which is time as experienced by human beings who are limited to experiencing the moments of time successively and thus cannot know the future as already existing. Stannard argues that God presumably views time objectively from eternity which is beyond time. He is both in time and beyond time and knows past, present and future simultaneously, akin

---

84. Cf. Pannenberg, "Eternity, Time and Space," 100.

85. Stannard, "God in and beyond Space and Time," 109–20.

to the block universe as employed in theoretical physics. If we accept the notion that to the Creator all points of created time are simultaneously present, and if we understand eternity as the togetherness of past, present and future, we can state that it is possible that the events of the Fall were a reality for God before it actually occurred in a human sense, and that God could have subjected creation to the distortive effects of the Fall, even before the human being was created. This would explain how death could exist before the Fall, but be at the same time a result of the Fall.

It is, furthermore, interesting that Scripture seems to understand history "forwards" and "backwards". Events are, at times, described as efficient although it hasn't occurred yet, or as having occurred already, but not being fully efficient as yet. There is thus not only a bouncing back in Scripture from the "already" to "not yet," but also a forwarding of events from "not yet" to "already." A few analogies will suffice: It is generally accepted in Reformed theology that Christ's atonement on the cross is not only effective for the sins of posteriority, but that the sins of the Old Covenant's members are also cleansed through his sacrifice. Even before Christ paid for the sins of the members of the Old Covenant, God grants them his grace because of Christ's work on the cross.[86] The atonement, though an historical event in time, has eternal significance and therefore applies "forwards" and "backwards". The same is true of God's election. It is said in Eph 1:4 that God's election of the faithful took place before creation in Christ. Even though neither Christ nor the faithful was born yet, the election of the faithful already took place in Christ as if Christ already paid for their sins. That which has not yet happen is already considered as effective. Christ's victory over evil is an example of precisely the opposite. Though Christ conquered evil on the cross, his victory is not as yet considered as efficient in the comprehensive sense. We still encounter the effects of sin and death. The full benefits of his victory will only be attained with the coming of the new heaven and earth. Thus, something that has already happened in time and space is not considered as fully efficient yet.

I suggest that the Fall, as is the case with the atonement, could be understood as an event in time, but with significance for past and present. We find in the creation narratives a mixture of poetic, prosaic and

86. Cf. Hebrews 11.

metaphorical language that do not narrate historical events in a chronological order, but describe a theological line of development from order to disorder, harmony to disharmony. This does not mean that the creation narratives are not "historical". It is history told in a non-historical genre. God did create, He did enter into a covenant with humanity and there was a Fall that occurred when humankind broke their covenant relationship with God. Even though the Fall was a historical event, which is described in the creation narratives through the use of metaphors, its effects could have been efficient before it took place. Death and suffering can therefore be regarded as the consequences of the Fall, even though their existence, precede the historical event of the Fall. Such an approach would be truer to Scripture than the "Irenaean" type of theodicy that has no option but to reject certain Scriptural teachings on creation and sin. It would also address some of the challenges that evolution poses to Christianity, because the defective and brutal aspects of evolution can then be understood as effects of sin. Furthermore, it would make the supra-lapsarian versus infralapsarian debate obsolete.

Evolution and Providence

The phenomenon of evolution begs the question whether we can speak of a creation that is completed as the Biblical creation narratives teaches. Though the notion of *creatio continua* is well known in Reformed theology, it has generally been understood in relation to God's original creative work and not so much in relation to God's providence. In my view, the Augustinian theological tradition should take the notion of a *creatio continua*, first introduced by Schleiermacher, much more seriously in its doctrine on providence. An understanding of *creatio continua ex nihilo* would contradict the evidence of Scripture that God completed His creation at a definite stage. However, *creatio continua* could also be related to God's providential care and his recreative work. As stated earlier, God is both in time and beyond time. He knows at every moment the past, present and future of the cosmic process and orders each successive event within the space-time continuum in terms of its impact on the cosmic process as a whole. The aim of His creation though, as Pannenberg rightly states, is obtainable only in time. Time is a necessary requirement for the formation of finite beings and a condition for the independent existence of His creatures. God gives creatures a span of time to organize their own being and acquire a more differentiated form of existence.[87] God's continuous reign over the cosmos and his sustenance of creation thus involves more than a mere preservation of the *status quo*, it also entails renewal in creation itself, dynamic progress in natural and cultural processes, and the development of human history towards God's eschatological purpose. A static creation would be capable of no history, evolution or progress, it would revolve around itself. *Creatio continua*, in contrast, encapsulates the Biblical understanding that the creation is eschatologically oriented to the future of God, which is the destiny of His creatures and is identical with His eternal present.

The difference between God original creative acts and his *creatio continua* would be that the first calls for the origination of things into existence from nothing, whereas the *creatio continua*, amongst other things, entails the continuous evolvement of things from simpler forms to increasing complexity. Such an understanding of the *creatio continua* would not contradict scriptural evidence on the original creation, it would give new depth to the Reformed doctrine of providence and recreation, and it would take the existence of biological and cultural evolution seriously. But then we must not isolate the notion of a *creatio continua* from the effects of sin. God's providential reign through *creatio continua* is also characterised by a continuous struggle with sin, suffering, chaos, the malfunctioning of evolutionary systems and randomness. The pain and suffering that co-incides with evolution is not part of a divine soulmaking scheme, but these processes are like all other worldy phenomena also contaminated by sin. Despite this, God is stronger than sin and will reach His overarching purposes with creation.

Conclusion

Though the classical "Augustinian" type of theodicy is based on an outdated worldview and also contains an inherent tension between the inevitability of sin and human accountability, there is no need to for Reformed scholars to replace the Augustinian paradigm with an "Irenaean" type of theodicy. Weaknesses within the Augustinian paradigm can be resolved without any drastic changes to the basic tenets of

---

87. Pannenberg, "Eternity, Time and Space," 104.

the Augustinian paradigm. This chapter proposes that Reformed theology rethinks its traditional linear concept of history and that it considers the possibility that the Fall could be an event within time, but with an eternal significance, that works both "backwards" and "forwards." Reformed theology could also deepen its doctrine of providence by making use of the dynamic notion of "*creatio continua.*"

3

Original Sin[1]

Introduction

THE TERM *ORIGINAL SIN* IS NOT FOUND IN SCRIPTURE, BUT WAS DEVEL-
oped by Augustine to articulate the biblical doctrine of the total depravity of humankind. He used the Latin term *peccatum originale* to explain
that the whole of humankind partakes in the original sin of Adam, and
consequently shares a common state of guilt before God.

Augustine's doctrine was accepted by the Council of Trent and the
Reformation, though not in all its aspects, in order to defend the doctrine of the total depravity of humankind and the undeserved nature of
the grace of God against the teachings of the Pelagians.

Recent studies of Calvin's use of Augustine established that
Augustine was Calvin's main source of inspiration and reference within
the Christian tradition.[2] Calvin's discussions of sin indeed reflect and
appeal directly to key positions advanced by Augustine, particularly
in his anti-Pelagian writings.[3] He followed Augustine in viewing sin as
more than a mere instance of negativity, but as a depravity that con-
taminates all dimensions of human existence. Yet it would be a mistake
to equate Augustine's view with that of Calvin. Though Calvin accepted
Augustine's doctrine of original sin and the bondage of the human
will, he also attempted to modify it in such a way that it would be logically more comprehensible. This chapter will discuss Calvin's attempt

---

1. This chapter was originally published as "Calvin's Modification of Augustine's
Doctrine on Original Sin," *In die Skriflig* 44.3 (2010) 71–89. Permission has been
granted by the editor.

2. Pitkin, "Nothing but Concupiscence," 347.

3. Ibid., 348.

to modify Augustine's doctrine on original sin. In the first section, Augustine's concept of original sin will be analysed. The second section will discuss Calvin's attempt to modify Augustine's doctrine, while the third section will reflect on the significance of Calvin's noetic approach to original sin.

Augustine's Understanding of Original Sin

Augustine's classical doctrine of original sin was the result of his negation of both Manichaeism and Pelagianism. Against the Manichaeans he maintained that evil is not identifiable with human finitude nor is it an ontological necessity, but erupts freely and contingently. Against the Pelagians he stated that sin is not merely accidental or contingent, but is a corruption of human nature because of the positive propensity of the will towards evil.[4]

The Manichaeans offered a deterministic account of sin that exempted the self from moral agency.[5] According to the Manichaeans God is in no way, whether directly or indirectly, the source of evil. Evil is rather an ontological force that stems from Matter that opposes the divine and compels the innately good souls of human beings to sin.[6] The Manichaeans thereby eliminated the moral dimension of evil and the personal accountability of the human being. As stated in chapter 2, Augustine insisted against the Manichaeans that evil is not an independent force or structural reality, but the corruption of being and moral goodness. It is committed by moral agents who possess a free will and are responsible for their own actions. Because God created human beings as good, God is in no way the source of evil or the creator of human sin.[7] He also does not act unjustly when he holds humanity to account for their sins. As noted earlier, Augustine was able to reconcile his position that humans are accountable for their sins with the view that God is not the source of evil, through the concept of the free will of the human.

However, after 392 AD, in his polemic against Fortunatus and the Pelagians, Augustine shifted the free exercise of will from all human

---

4. Cf. Duffy, "Our Hearts of Darkness," 600. Augustine, "De Civitate Dei," XII.

5. Babcock, "Augustine on Sin," 30.

6. Bonner, St Augustine of Hippo, 317. Babcock, "Augustine on Sin," 31.

7. Augustine, "De Civitate Dei," XII.

beings to only the first human being.[8] Because of the first human's initial sin the whole of humankind descended into the necessity of habit
and bondage to sin and death. After the first sin, humankind sins involuntarily. Yet Augustine maintained that though there is complicity
from the start, a subsequent set of forced actions can still be interpreted
as the agent's own. God's penalty on humanity's sin is therefore justly
imposed.[9]

Contrary to Augustine, Pelagius understood grace to be either
a natural faculty or a form of illumination after baptism has cleansed
sin. The human's natural faculties are good because they are created
by the good Creator, therefore the human could, if he or she chose, be
without sin. Though people's wills are sound, their minds are clouded
and they therefore need the illumination of the Law and Gospel to lead
a Christian life after the remission of sins through baptism.[10] Closely
connected with Pelagius's view on grace was a particular doctrine of
the Fall which denied that Adam's sin injured his descendants or can
be transmitted to subsequent generations. Adam's sin only injured himself, and though he set an evil example for his descendants, he did not
corrupt their nature also. Human nature cannot be corrupted by sin,
because sin is an action, not a substance, and therefore cannot change
our nature.[11] Every descendant of Adam possesses Adam's original innocence and thus there is no such thing as original sin.[12]

Augustine found Pelagius's reduction of sin to a conscious free
choice simplistic. He held that sin not only amounts to an option for
another mode of being, but to the disintegration of that nature.[13] In
De Natura et Gratia he states that man initially had a free will but that
original sin darkened and flawed man's will so that human nature itself
is corrupted:

> Man's nature, indeed, was created at first faultless and without
> any sin; but that nature of man in which everyone is born from
> Adam, now wants the Physician because it is not sound. All

---

8. Cf Augustine, *Acta seu Disputatio*, XXII. Babcock, "Augustine on Sin," 40.

9. Cf Augustine, *Acta seu Disputatio*, XXII. Babcock, "Augustine on Sin," 38.

10. Bonner, *St Augustine of Hippo*, 362.

11. Augustine, "De Natura et Gratia," XIX.

12. Cf. Bonner, *St Augustine of Hippo*, 318–19.

13. Cf. Duffy, "Our Hearts of Darkness," 602.

good qualities, no doubt, which it still possesses in its make, life, senses, intellect it has of the Most High God, its Creator and Maker. But the flaw which darkens and weakens all those natural goods, so that it has need of illumination and healing, it has not contracted from its blameless Creator—but from that original sin, which it committed by free will.[14]

For his position to be intelligible, he had to give some indication of how the sin of the first human beings is continuous with the character of subsequent generations. Otherwise he could not maintain the position that sin is genuinely the moral agent's own. In *De Civitate Dei*[15] he argues that the Fall differs from the ordinary daily sin of the human in that it leads to a shift in the orientation of the will from God to the self.

Augustine regards pride, which is a longing for a perverse kind of exaltation, as the start of every kind of sin. As a result of his pride humankind decided to desert God, who is the changeless Good, to follow its own desire. In doing so, the human abandons the light and love of God. This, in turn, causes a darkening of the human will and a taking of itself rather than God as the principle of existence.[16] As noted in chapter 2, the Fall led, according to Augustine, to the weakening of all humankind's faculties so that they become liable to disease, unable to rule the desires of the body, and subject to death.[17]

However, two questions needed to be answered: Firstly, how did the original evil act arise? Secondly, how is the sin of the first human beings transmitted to subsequent generations?

In *De Civitate Dei*[18] Augustine attempts to answer the first question by stating that whereas the first evil deed had an efficient cause, evil will had no efficient cause, because nothing causes an evil will, since it is the evil will itself which causes the evil act. Anything that one might suppose to cause an evil will must have a will of itself. That will must be

14. "Natura quipped hominis primitus inculpate et sine ullo vitio create est, naturo vero ista hominis, qua unusquisque ex Adam nascitur, jam medico indigent, qui sana non est. Omnia quidem bona, quae habet informatione, vita sensibus, mente a summon Deo habet creatore et artifice suo. Vitium vero, quod ista naturalia bona contenebrat et infirmat, ut illuminatione et curatione opus habeat, non ab inculpabili artifice contractum est, sed ex originali peccato, quod commisum est libero arbitrio" (iii).

15. Augustine, "De Civitate Dei," XIV.12.

16. Ibid., XIV.3.

17. Augustine, "De Perfectione Justitiae," II.

18. Augustine, "De Civitate Dei," XII.6.

either good or bad. If it is good it would be absurd to think that a good will can cause evil—if it is evil the question remains, what caused that evil will? An evil will that is caused by an evil will cannot be the first act of evil. If it is replied that it had no cause and had always existed, the question is whether it existed in nature. If it was not in nature, then it did not exist at all. If it existed in some nature, it vitiated that nature and corrupted it. A bad will cannot exist in a bad nature, but only in a good but mutable nature that can be corrupted. Therefore an evil will could not exist eternally in anything, because an evil will needs the goodness of nature to destroy it. If the evil will was not eternally there, who created it? The only possible answer is: Something that had no will. However, this answer is unsatisfactory, because if such a being is equal or superior to angelic nature it must have a will, and that will must be good. A nature without will or with an evil will cannot be regarded as equal to a nature endowed with a good will.

Augustine's conclusion is that evil resides in none other than the will's own turning from God, that desires the inferior thing in a perverted and inordinate manner. This turning of the will is not a matter of efficiency but of deficiency, because the evil will is not effective but defective.[19] To defect from Him who is the Supreme Existence, to something less real, is to begin to have an evil will. To try to discover the causes of defection is like trying to see darkness or hear silence. Evil cannot exist on its own and is not intellectually comprehensible. Sin is the perverse manifestation of our godlike faculty of freedom.[20]

In *De Civitate Dei*[21] Augustine states that the angelic fall, which preceded the human fall, was a defection whose causes were lacking. Since the angels were created, it follows that their wills also had to be created. The good angels received their wills from God. The evil angels were created good but became evil through their own bad will. This came about through a voluntary falling away from the good so that their evil nature is not caused by the good but by a falling away from good. The reason why some angels fell away and others not lies in the fact that those who fell away received less grace of the divine love than others who continued in that grace, or, if both groups of angels were

---

19. Augustine, "De Civitate Dei," XII.7.

20. Cf. Mathewes, "Augustinian Anthropology," 205.

21. Augustine, "De Civitate Dei," XII.9.

created equal, the one group fell through their evil will, while the others had greater help to enable them to attain the fullness of bliss. Augustine thus attributes the first cause of evil not only to an absence of cause but also to the absence of divine grace.

Babcock[22] rightly observes that Augustine's explanation does not solve the problem. If the first evil will is simply uncaused, it will have the status of an entirely accidental happening and will no more count as the agent's own than it would be if it could be ascribed to an efficient cause. Secondly, it is difficult to see how a defection can be described as a defect if it is not an act at all.

With regard to the question of the transmission of the original sin to subsequent generations, Augustine held that original sin is both an inherited guilt (*reatum*) and inherited disease (*vitium*). The *reatus* of sin denotes its juridical aspect whereby it is a violation of God's law and therefore punishable, while the *vitium* is the corruption and crippling effect of sin on human nature.[23] He grounded his view on the Latin translation of Rom 5:12 which says:

> Therefore, just as sin entered this world by one man and through sin death; so death passed into all men, in whom all sinned.[24]

On the basis of this translation of Rom 5:12 he posits the seminal identity of the human race with Adam. In *De Peccatorum Meritis et Remissione*[25] he correspondingly states that the condemnation of Adam's progeny was constituted in Adam. From one man all people were born to a state of condemnation from which there is no deliverance, but through the Saviour's grace.

According to Bonner[26] Augustine clearly asserts that all future generations were in some sense present in their progenitor's loins at the time of the Fall, and therefore all humankind participated, in some mysterious fashion, in the original sin of Adam.

However, Augustine made a serious mistake in his exegesis of Rom 5:12 by using a wrong Latin translation of Rom 5:12. The Greek

22. Babcock, "Augustine on Sin," 46.

23. Duffy, "Our Hearts of Darkness," 603.

24. Per unum hominem peccatum intravit in mundum et per peccatum mors, et ita in omnes hominess pertransiit, in quo omnes peccaverunt.

25. Augustine, "De Peccatorum Meritis et Remissione," I:12.

26. Bonner, *St Augustine of Hippo*, 372.

formulation reads: *epi hō pantes ēmarton* not *en hō*. In other words, humankind does not sin *in Adam* but *because of Adam*. This mistake casts serious doubts upon Augustine's doctrine on the transmission of sin.

Augustine locates the transmission of sin from the first human beings to subsequent generations in concupiscence. Adam's disobedience to God caused him to lose the power to control his body. This loss of power over the body becomes particularly evident in the human's sexual desire. In *De Civitate Dei*[27] he states that humans possessed no shame about their nakedness before the Fall, because lust did not yet rouse their sexual members independently of their decisions. After the Fall humans became ashamed of their nakedness, because they lost control over their members and sexual desires, so that lust—that is concupiscence—arose.[28]

For Augustine, concupiscence is that element of lust which is inseparable from fallen sexuality.[29] Though Augustine does not disparage matrimony and respects it as an institution of God, even Christian marriage contains the sickness of concupiscence, because generation cannot be effected without the ardour of lust.[30] Through marriage two things are propagated, namely nature that is good, and the vice of nature that is evil. It is through concupiscence, then, that the guilt (*reatum*) and disease (*vitium*) of original sin are conveyed from parents to their children.[31]

Christ alone, who was born from the virgin Mary through the operation of the Holy Spirit, is free from original sin, because concupiscence was not involved in His conception and birth. He can therefore offer a sacrifice for the sins of humankind.[32]

Because of their inherited guilt, all men who are born by human generation form a lump of sin (*massa peccati, luti, perditionis*), justly

27. Augustine, "De Civitate Dei," XIV.17.

28. Augustine, "De Civitate Dei," XIV.16.

29. Cf. Bonner, *St Augustine of Hippo*, 377.

30. Augustine, "De Nuptiis et Concupiscentia," I:29.

31. Ibid., I:24.

32. Ibid.:

> ex hac, inquam, concupiscentia carnis, tanquam filia peccati, et quando illi ad turpia consentitur, etiam peccatorum matre multorum, quacumque nascitur proles, originali est obligate peccato nisi in illo renascutur, quem sine ista concupiscentia Virgo concepit: propterea quando nasci est in carne dignatus, sine peccato solus est natus.

deserve damnation, even if they commit no sins to add to the guilt they inherited, unless they are cleansed by baptism. Though baptism remits the guilt of concupiscence, concupiscence remains in the regenerate, because semination takes place through concupiscence. Yet baptism remits carnal concupiscence in the regenerate, not so that it is put out of existence, but so that it is not imputed to sin.[33]

In summary, Augustine's doctrine on original sin is as follows: The human was created with a free will, which means that human nature was created with the possibility, but not the necessity to sin. The Fall of the human lead to a redirection of the human's will away from the God to the world and its changeable, finite goods causing people to lose their original free will and to become enslaved to sin. This falling-away of human will was an unexplainable act whose cause is deficient—for there is no cause. Desire, a natural tendency, becomes after the Fall an enslaving concupiscence. The original sin of Adam is transmitted to subsequent generations through sexual concupiscence, since procreation cannot take place without lust.

Clearly the Manichaeans pushed Augustine to historicise evil, while the Pelagians led him to amplify the consequences of Adam's historical act to the point of turning the present chain of freedom into a fatality.[34] In his effort to counter the views of both the Manicheans and Pelagians Augustine mixed juridical and biological categories in his perspective on original sin. This made his doctrine appear incoherent and caused an epistemological question that subsequent theologians in the Augustinian tradition had to address, namely: How can humans be held responsible for their sins, if sin is an inevitable inherited condition? This question has far-reaching implications because it pertains to the relationship between human moral agency and God's sovereignty. How can human freedom and divine sovereignty be affirmed at the same time?

---

33. Augustine, "De Nuptiis et Concupiscentia," I:25:
    Dimitti concupiscentiam carnis in baptismo, non ut non sit, sed ut inpeccatum non imputetur.
34. Duquoc, "New Approaches to Original Sin," 193.

Calvin's Perspective on Original Sin

Calvin's central interest, around which his theological work was orga-
nized, was to demonstrate and maintain the glory of God. In order to
display this vision of the glory of God Calvin used the human race as
a foil: all human faculties are vitiated and corrupted and human works
are therefore useless for purposes of salvation. The insignificance of the
human being is the exaltation of God.[35] Knowledge of God and of the
self is therefore of utmost importance for achieving a consciousness
of the glory of God. This theological premise provides the impetus for
Calvin's doctrine on original sin. Pitkin[36] rightly notes that Calvin shifts
the focus of the debate on original sin to his own chief concern: knowledge of God and self.

The first difference between Calvin and Augustine concerns
Calvin's noetic approach to original sin. Whereas Augustine located the
first sin in pride, Calvin ascribes it to the human's longing for illicit
knowledge. Original sin denotes a change of the mind. The sin of the
first couple is best understood not as pride but as unbelief that both
male and female shared.[37] Calvin's difference with Augustine on the nature of the first sin is important. By underscoring the essentially noetic
character of the first sin he shifts the focus away from the role of the will
in the Fall. Though the will was involved in the Fall and defected with
the mind, Calvin emphasises the role of the mind. Original sin is, along
with a misdirected will, a failure to know God and self. The mind's corruption is not only moral in nature, but it is a fundamental religious
blindness. Although true knowledge of God is revealed through nature,
the conscience and the sense of the divinity, the fallen mind fails to
receive this knowledge and is with respect to God filled with boundless
confusion.[38]

Calvin's emphasis on original sin as a corruption of the mind and
the will is not in the same intellectual tradition as the Augustinian one.[39]
Augustine understands sin to be concupiscence. The fallen will lacks
the power to achieve the good that the intellect knows. Calvin, how-

---

35. Miles, "Theology, Anthropology, and the Human Body," 304.

36. Pitkin, "Nothing but Concupiscence," 349.

37. Calvin, *Genesis*, 152–53.

38. Cf. Pitkin, "Nothing but Concupiscence," 360, 365.

39. Ibid., 360.

ever, intensifies the problem of sin by stating that the mind itself no longer knows the good to be done. This different understanding of sin is largely due to a different understanding of human nature.

According to Calvin[40] the human being consists of a body and a soul. The soul is the nobler part and the primary seat of the divine image, while the body is simply the habitation of the soul. The image of God is manifested in the soul by light of intellect, while the body is a reflection of the dynamics of the soul:

> Hence although the soul is not the man, there is no absurdity in holding that he is called image of God in respect of the soul. . . . By the term image of God is denoted the integrity with which Adam was endued when his intellect was clear, his affections subordinated to reason, all his senses duly regulated, and when he truly ascribed all his excellence to the admirable gifts of the Maker. And though the primary sea of the divine image was in the mind and the heart, or in the soul and its powers, there was no part even of the body in which some rays of glory did not shine . . . at the beginning the image of God was manifested by light of intellect, rectitude of heart, and soundness of every part.[41]

The Fall, however, led to a weakening of the soul's capacity to maintain the integrity of body and soul.[42] Thus in contrast to Augustine, who locates the effects of sin in the human's loss of control of his or her physical desires, Calvin locates the crippling effects of the corruption of the image in the soul. According to Calvin the taint of sin resides in the flesh and the spirit. The flesh—which must not be equated with the human body—designates in Calvin's thought the whole human be-

---

40. Calvin, *Inst*. 1.15.2.

41. Ibid., 1.15.3:

> Quamvis ergo anima non sit homo, absurdum tamen non est, eum animae respectu vocari Dei imaginem: etsi principium quod nuper posui retineo, patere Dei effigiem ad totam preastantiam, qua eminet hominis natura inter omnes animantium species. Proinde hac voce notatur integritas, qua preaditus fuit Adam quum recta intelligentia polleret, affectus haberet compositos ad rationem sensus omnes recto ordine temperatos, vereque eximiis dotibus opificis sui excellentiam referret. Ac quamvis primaria sedes divinae imaginis fuerit in mente et corde, vel in animae eiusque potentiis: nulla tamen pars fuit etiam usque ad corpus in qua non scintillae aliquae micarent.

42. Ibid., 1.15.6.

ing in the condition of sinfulness. It is the governing aspect of human nature.[43] "Flesh" is an attitude of mind alienated from God, which uses and abuses the body and the soul.[44] The soul participates in the flesh more than the body does, because when Scripture says that the human must be born again it refers to the soul not the body. The body cannot be reborn.[45] In Calvin's thought the body plays no role either in the corruption of the soul or in its own corruption, but it is the helpless victim of the destructive hegemony of the flesh. It is the mind and its potential consciousness of the glory of God that interests Calvin. The body has no potential for consciousness—it is motion devoid of essence—in contrast to the soul, which is endowed with essence and can be quickened.[46]

These different understandings of the essential nature of the human being lead to different understandings of the mode of the transmission of original sin. Augustine's view of human nature leads him to believe that all human beings are in a physical solidarity with Adam, and hence when he sinned, all sinned and were guilty. Though Calvin defines sin as a hereditary corruption in all parts of the human being, he does not use Augustine's biological categories to explain original sin and the transmission thereof. In his commentary on Psalm 51 Calvin states that the question on the transmission of sins from Adam to subsequent generations is not important and that it is not sensible to enter into such mysterious discussions (*labyrinthos*).[47]

In his comments on Genesis 3:7 Calvin subtly rejects the Augustinian view that ashamedness and the stirrings of sexual concupiscence were the first effects of the Fall.[48] Instead he emphasizes the noetic effects of the Fall. By eating the fruit Adam and Eve's eyes were opened and they experienced a confused sense of evil. It is thus not sexual concupiscence, but rather the damage done to the human mind and will that are the first effects of the Fall.

43. Ibid., 2.3.1.

44. Cf. Miles, "Theology, Anthropology, and the Human Body," 312.

45. Calvin, *Inst.* 2.3.1.

46. Cf. Miles, "Theology, Anthropology, and the Human Body," 314, 317.

47. Calvin, *Commentary on the Book of Psalms*, 291.

48. Calvin, *Genesis*, 158–59.

In the *Institutes*[49] he dispenses with Augustine's views on the role of sexual desire in the transmission of sins and locates the reason for humankind's guilt in God's ordination:

> The cause of the contagion is neither in the substance of the flesh nor the soul, but God was pleased to ordain that those gifts which he had bestowed on the first man, that man should lose as well for his descendants as for himself.[50]

Calvin's position on the transmission of sin, that it is not the mode of conception but the divine decree that accounts for the propagation of sin, necessarily leads him to reject Augustine's view on the meaning of Christ's virgin birth. Whereas Augustine located Christ's sinlessness in him being conceived without sexual desire, Jesus was, according to Calvin, free of sin, not because of the virginal conception, but because he was sanctified by the Spirit. According to Calvin it is childish trifling to maintain that Christ is free from all taint, because he was not begotten through the seed of a man. Would that imply that the woman is not impure? Christ was not free of all taint, merely because he was born of a woman unconnected with a man, but because he was sanctified by the Spirit, so that the generation was pure and spotless, such as it would have been before Adam's fall.[51]

The second important difference between Calvin and Augustine lies in Calvin's approach to God's role in the Fall. In his commentary on Genesis he does not attempt to provide a precise description of the Fall, but to explain how it was possible that the original human nature could fall. He states that God not only permitted but indeed ordained the Fall. First he states that evil is not from nature, but from defection,

49. Calvin, *Inst.* 2.1.7.

50. Neque enim in substantia carnis aut animae causam habet contagio: sed quia a Deo ita fuit ordinatum, ut quae primo homini dona contulerat, ille tam sibi quam suis haberet simul ac perderet.

51. Calvin, *Inst.* 2.13.4:

> Quod etiam pro absurdo nobis obtrudunt, si Sermo Dei carnem induit, fuisse igitur angusto terreni corporis ergastulo inclusum, mera est procacitas: quia etsi in unam personam coaluit immense Verbi essential cum natura hominis, nullam tamen inclusionem fingimus. Mirabiliter enim e coelo descendit Filius Dei, ut coelum tamen non relinqueret: mirabiliter in utero Virginis gestari, in terries versari, et in cruce pendere voluit, ut simper mundum impleret, sicut ab initio.

and that Adam fell into sin through his own fault.[52] Yet Adam did not fall without the will and ordination of God since the created character of the first human being's will makes such a defection possible.[53] In his comments on Genesis 3:7[54] he states even more clearly that God created man to be flexible, and not only permitted, but willed that he should be tempted.

Calvin, therefore, differs fundamentally with Augustine on the origin of evil. Whereas Augustine went to great lengths to explain that God was not the origin of evil, and that evil is an unexplainable phenomenon that has no cause, Calvin attributes evil and sin to God's eternal decree.[55] According to Calvin God's decrees of election and reprobation are not due to the Fall but were made before it, and without regard to it, while Augustine is of the view that we are condemned because we fell in Adam, who sinned by the abuse of the free will. God foresaw the Fall but did not compel it.[56]

In summary, Calvin shares Augustine's view that original sin is an inheritance and that the whole of human nature is contaminated by it. Yet there are also substantial differences between Augustine and Calvin's view. Augustine went to considerable effort to explain that sin does not find its origin in God. God foresaw the Fall but did not compel it. Calvin located sin in God's eternal decree and permission. Whereas Augustine formulated his view to counter the Manichaeans and Pelagians, Calvin shifted the focus in his doctrine on original sin to knowledge of God and the self. The result was that he emphasized the noetic character of sin as moral and religious blindness. His view of the body as motion devoid of essence, made him depart from Augustine's view that the original sin is transmitted biologically to subsequent generations through sexual desire. According to Calvin sin is not transmitted through conception, but because of God's divine decree. These different positions on the transmission of original sin culminated in different understandings of the meaning of Christ's virgin birth. Augustine believed that Jesus was born free of sin, because of a conception without sexual desire, whereas

52. Calvin, *Genesis*, 142.
53. Ibid., 144.
54. Ibid., 158.
55. Cf. ibid.
56. Cf. Bonner, *St Augustine of Hippo*, 387.

Calvin believed that Jesus was born free of sin because he was sanctified by the Spirit.

Problems with the Augustinian Position

The Augustinian doctrine of original sin remains one of the most controversial doctrines in theology. The main critique against it pertains to its understanding of the personal accountability of the human being. It is often described as a fatalistic dogma that ascribes guilt to one person because of the sin of another individual. If sin is inherited and therefore an involuntarily act, humankind cannot be held responsible for their sins and God would therefore be unjust to punish humankind for their sins. Punishment because of an inherited guilt is not reconcilable with God's righteousness. To ascribe guilt to one person because of the guilt of another would, according to critics, defy the essence of justice.[57] It is also alleged that the doctrine is logically inconsistent. On the one hand original sin is by definition an inherited corruption, or at least an inevitable one, yet it is also regarded as not belonging to humankind's essential nature and therefore is not outside the realm of their responsibility.[58]

The problem with Augustine's classical doctrine on original sin is that it is based upon a literal historical interpretation of Genesis 1–3, which causes a set of related problems. These chapters were thought to yield divinely inspired and infallible historical data about creation, the state of innocence and the Fall.[59] The result of this literal approach was that the origin of evil was attributed to a literal first couple, the universality of sin was grounded in the monogenistic[60] unity of all humankind and biological terms was used to explain original sin. The majority of biblical scholarship in the last half century is of the opinion that it is not the purpose of Genesis 1–3 to present us with history in the scientific sense of the word. Genesis 1, in my view, does not present itself as literal history, but contains a mixture of prosaic and poetic material. Though Genesis 1 is characterized by the absence of synonymous and antithetical parallelisms, it contains patterned repetitions, rhythm, symmetrical structures and prolonged syntactically parallel sentence constructions.

57. Cf. Berkouwer, *Sin*, 426. Rees, "Anxiety of Inheritance," 77.

58. Cf. Niebuhr, *Nature and Destiny of Man*, 257.

59. Cf. Duffy, "Our Hearts of Darkness," 207.

60. Monogenism is the view that all people descent from one human being.

Days 1 and 4, 2 and 5, 3 and 6 are brought into relation with each other in a very skilled, artistic manner.

Besides the abovementioned, the Genesis narratives also have a distinctly theological and polemic purpose. They use symbols and metaphors to explain the relationship between God, the cosmos, humans and evil. They emphasize over and against Canaanite and Babylonian creation myths that God is the only God, that nothing in creation itself is divine, that humankind does not owe its origin to the gods, that nature is the creation of God, and nature and humankind are not ruled by chaotic powers. Questions on whether Adam is the physical father of all people, if his sin alone causes deprivation of grace in all and whether this deprivation was transmitted by physical generation, move far beyond the data and original intention of the creation narratives. Their intention rather is to indicate that God created His creation to be good, that sin does not find its origin in God, but in the human being, and that the sinfulness of humankind is systemic in nature.

Though Calvin's approach to the creation narratives was also strictly literal and his understanding of particularly the origin of evil not without problems, his noetic approach to original sin, might be helpful in solving the tension—inherent in Augustine's doctrine on original sin—between the inevitability of sin and man's responsibility for sin. The usefulness of a noetic approach is that it enables us to stress both the historical and natural dimension of original sin. Original sin denotes a condition of religious and moral blindness. This condition originated in the alienation that occurred between God and humankind, because of humankind's disobedience of the covenant of God. Where God is absent, sin enters, in the same way that darkness enters where light is absent. A condition of perfectness can, after all, only exist where humankind stands in full communion with God. The disobedience of humankind has brought alienation and separation, and with them, depravity. God is not the source of sin, but humankind is, because humankind separated itself from God who is the source of all goodness. The resulting condition of blindness affects all dimensions of human existence, also the human's material and biological existence. Yet, the biological nature is not per se the locus of sin, as Augustine tends to believe. With regard to sin and generation Bavinck[61] states the following:

> De erfzonde is nog iets anders, wat heden ten dage onder heri-diteit wordt verstaan. Immers is zij geen soorteienschap, die tot het wezen des menschen behoort, want zij is door overtreding van Gods gebod in de menschelijke natuur ingekomen en kan er door wedergeboorte en heiligmaking weder uit weggenomen wordt; en zij is ter andere zijde ook geen individuëele verwor-vene eigenschap, want zij is alle menschen zonder uitzondering eigen.

Bavinck then proceeds to define sin ethically:

> De erfzonde is toch geen substantie, die zetelt in het liggaam en door generatie kan worden overgeplant; zij is een zedelijke qualiteit van de mens, die de gemeenschap met God mist, welke hij naar zijn oorspronklijke natuur bezitten moest en bezeten heft.[62]

The alienation between man and God causes a condition of human and natural depravity wherein everything is led astray and therefore threatened by a return to chaos. The flood narrative explains the consequences of the Fall as a return to its original watery chaos. Only through the redemptive works of God can humankind make a new beginning. Because the human is morally and religiously blind he is unable to enter freely into a relationship with God and to love God by his own natural powers. This natural inability exists prior to the choice of a given individual.

Despite God's redemptive work the effects of the Fall remain. Humankind's natural depravity is transmitted through procreation in the sense that it is through procreation alone that man enters into human history that is bound with evil. To be in the world is to be in the condition of original sin—that is, a condition of moral and religious blindness, since the communication of ethical and religious values is interrupted through the sins of previous generations. Original sin is not mere imitation, but is part of human nature, since we are born with a religious blindness which is the result of humankind's alienation from God.

---

61. Bavinck, *Gereformeerde Dogmatiek*, 96.
62. Bavinck, *Gereformeerde Dogmatiek*, 97.

Duffy's[63] description of original sin, that underscores the above-mentioned perspective, is in my view the most substantial:

> Being situated in and participating in the sin of the world is not
> a conscious decision. It is not *imitatione*. For sin works its shap-
> ing influence before one is capable of moral decisions. Inserted
> into a race and environment contaminated by corporate evil,
> each person is affected by the contagion before being able to
> offer the least resistance.

The universal nature of sin implies that humankind's guilt is both collective and personal in nature. It is collective in the sense that humankind's history of sin constitutes a whole that has a historic dimension. Because of humankind's moral blindness, sin entered into the world and inhabits the world, it intervenes, it abounds and it reigns.[64] Humankind is thus historically bound with evil and accountable to God for its disobedience to the covenant of God. The guilt of original sin is not passed down to subsequent generations through natural descent, but is attributed to subsequent generations by God because original sin is not merely a sin of one forefather, but is a collective sin continuously committed by the whole of humanity. Sin is not a physical inheritance, but it is inevitable because the human being lives outside true communion with God and therefore in a state of religious and moral blindness. Though Christ came to restore the relationship between God and the human, we still live in the state of tension between the *yet* and *not yet* of the kingdom of God. The reconciliation that Christ brought has restored the relationship between God and the human in part, but not completely. Full communion between God and the human will only be realised at the *parousia*.

The unity of humankind in sin is not a physical unity but a theological unity. God takes all humankind to be the sinner that is Adam. Humankind's sin is not the act of Adam, but the sin of Adam is the act of humankind. God is not unfair in imputing guilt to the whole of humankind because the condition of original sin is a condition of generic human nature.[65] Though the human cannot be held responsible for something he inherited—because inheritance designates that which

---

63. Duffy, "Our Hearts of Darkness," 615–16.

64. Ibid., 616.

65. Cf. Psalm 51.

precedes the individual and for which he cannot account—he can be held responsible for actions that he freely chose even if it is inevitable that he will make the wrong choice.[66] Because the human lives outside true communion with God and therefore in a state of religious blindness, he inevitably asserts his freedom in the wrong way. Since human actions can be both inevitable as well as freely chosen, the human is really and truly guilty of the sin of Adam.[67] The relationship between inevitability and responsibility is thus not contradictory but rather dialectical in nature.

Romans 5 provides an important perspective in this regard. Adam and Christ are seen as representatives of different *aeons*. Paul, thereby, emphasizes that God's grace in Adam reigns over the power of sin in Adam. Paul explains the universal culpability of humanity in Romans 5 Christologically and corporatively.[68] His didactic purpose in Romans 5 is not to affirm the existence of a unique sinner, but to emphasize the universal reach—though not universal efficiency—of redemption in Jesus Christ.[69] Paul does not see the sin of one human as the sin of all, but all as acting in the single individual who is representative of the group.[70]

This collective guilt would not have been if sin had not a personal dimension and if every human being was not an actual sinner. Sin is personal and actual in every human being in the sense that every person lives outside of a true personal relationship with God and therefore in a moral condition of sin. Sin is not only potentially part of the human, but actually so, since the human lives in the old aeon that is characterised by religious and moral blindness and a disturbed relationship with God.

Conclusion

The Christian doctrines of sin and grace were mostly developed in their decisive aspects from the perspective of Christology, not from the perspective of Genesis 1–3. Though the Old Testament says a great deal

66. Cf. Niebuhr, *Nature and Destiny of Man*, 66.

67. Cf. Rees, "Anxiety of Inheritance," 81.

68. Cf. Ridderbos, *Paulus: ontwerp van zijn theologie*, 60.

69. Ibid.

70. Cf. Berkouwer, *Sin*, 323.

about sin and grace, both of these were revealed in their deepest sense in Jesus Christ.[71] Knowledge of sin is produced by the Gospel, because it points out to us how much it cost God to redeem us. In the act by which the Gospel announces salvation in Jesus Christ to us, it reveals to us that sin is committed by human beings.[72]

The universal nature of Christ's redemptive work can only be attributed to the universal nature of sin. The sacrificial atonement of Christ was necessary only because man is guilty before God for his sins. That the human can be saved through grace alone can only be because the human is a slave of sin and incapable of salvaging himself. In essence, original sin denotes humankind's break with God which makes reconciliation in and through Christ necessary.

71. Cf. Lohse, *Short History of Christian Doctrine*, 101.

72. Berkouwer, *Sin*, 156.

4

The Nature of Christ's Atonement

The Historical Origin of Satisfaction Theory

ANSELM'S WORK *CUR DEUS HOMO* (1098) WAS THE FIRST SERIOUS attempt to set forth a comprehensive and systematic doctrine of atonement. His main aim was to provide an objective doctrine of atonement that would reject an idea of forgiveness of sin, which would on the one hand be a bare remission of penalty, and on the other an optimistic conception of the human being's capacity to perform all that is needed.[1] According to Anselm, sin offends the honor of God because it is in essence the failure to give God His due.[2] Sin also mars the beauty of the universe by disrupting the order and beauty of creation.[3] In order for God's honor to be kept intact, two possibilities exist: either a balancing of scales through retributive punishment, or satisfaction that remits the penalty through a means other than punishment.[4] Because God is holy, human guilt necessitates a sacrifice that is undefiled. However, humankind is unable to offer a sufficient sacrifice because no-one without sin exists. In addition, only the penalty of death is sufficient to restore God's honor, because it offers the greatest possible satisfaction.[5] A finite being's greatest compensation or offered satisfaction is at best finite, and cannot restore God's eternal dignity.[6] Atonement therefore needs to be sought by an eternal being who is greater than all things but God, but

1. Aulén, *Christus Victor*, 85.
2. Anselm, "Cur Deus Homo," 216.
3. Ibid., 223, 224.
4. Ibid., 216–17, 221.
5. Ibid., 245, 272.
6. Ibid., 246–47.

who is simultaneously truly human, since humans have to compensate for their own sins. The only person who can offer such a satisfaction is a God-man who partakes in human nature, but is not sinful.[7]

Anselm's doctrine shows similarities with the feudal philosophy of his time and with Neo-Platonism. God is depicted as a feudal overlord bound above all things to safeguard His honor and to demand adequate satisfaction for any infringement of it, while the universe is viewed as a hierarchic constellation of beauty that finds its prototype in divine nature.[8] These influences cause Anselm to focus on an abstract code of honor that functions apart from God's being. At the same time the notion of penalty for sin is not adequately expounded in his doctrine. Though Anselm is clear in saying that satisfaction is rendered through a payment in death, he is not clear about the exact relationship between guilt and punishment. In his book *Jesus Kurios*, Bram van Beek rightly critisizes the rational nature of Anselm's discourse. He notes that Anselm emphasizes the objective reality of guilt, but the relational aspect of reconciliation is underemphasized. Surely over and against God's wrath as an emotion stands not only rational payment in blood, but an equally emotional love that embraces the sinner. Furthermore, if Anselm's rational method is followed to its full conclusions several loopholes appear. Van de Beek asks: How is it that a finite human being can mar the glory of an infinite God? Anselm's view on sin and merit is also, according to Van de Beek, unbalanced. When it comes to human sin the infinite consequences are highlighted, while on the side of merit finitude is highlighted. Van de Beek rightly states that Anselm tends to see the human and divine natures of Christ in opposition to each other. For Anselm only the death of Jesus has real meaning. His life is necessary only to make it possible for Jesus to die as a divine human being. The *unio personalis* only become important in his death.[9]

Despite some shortcomings, Anselm provided a foundation that the Reformers later built on. While Anselm attempted to give a rational philosophical explanation of atonement, the Reformers were more concerned with the actual biblical data. They regarded the sacrificial and penal models that are found in Scripture as the unifying centre of

---

7. Ibid., 260.

8. Cf. James, "Atonement in Church History," 246.

9. Van de Beek, *Jesus Kurios*, 208–10.

the Christian doctrine of the atonement.[10] Whereas Anselm argues that offended honor calls for atonement, the Reformers changed the focus to offended righteousness.[11] They did not view sin in terms of dishonor, but in terms of guilt and punishment, *satisfaction poenalis* (satisfaction through punishment). In addition, the Reformers did not distinguish between either punishment or satisfaction, but rather believed that satisfaction takes place through punishment. God's justice demands that sin must be punished, hence the idea of penal substitution. It is penal in the sense that Christ's death is a penalty for sin, it is substitutionary in the sense that Christ served as a substitute sacrifice on behalf of sinners. Satisfaction does not merely result from the death of Christ, but from his voluntary and obedient fulfilment of God's law throughout His life in an active and passive sense. His incarnation and morally blameless life together with his vicarious penitence constitute one act of reparation sufficient to atone for the sin of fallen beings.[12] The Father accepts Christ's sacrifice because He loves His Son and has compassion for sinners. Though Christ is punished in the place of humanity, His sacrifice only becomes effective through the union of faith between the sinner and Christ, which is the result of the regenerative work of the Holy Spirit.

John Calvin understood Christ's death as a mysterious encounter between God's love and justice. He regarded God's love as the supreme motive behind God's work of redemption. In the second book of the 1559 edition of his *Institutes* Calvin describes his understanding of atonement in vivid terms of penal substitution combined with a strong sense of Christ as the source of God's love.[13]

Henri Blocher[14] notes that Calvin mainly uses two language sets when speaking about the atonement, namely the religious cultic language of sacrifice, with such terms as expiation, curse, propitiation, uncleanness and purification by means of the shedding of blood, and forensic or judicial language of condemnation, with terms such as guilt, imputation, judgment, penalty and remission. Clearly, Calvin

---

10. Cf. Van Asselt, "Christ's Atonement," 61.

11. Hannah, "Anselm on the Doctrine of Atonement," 342.

12. Cf. Calvin, *Inst.* 2.16.6.

13. Ibid., 2.16.2.

14. Blocher, "Atonement in John Calvin's Theology," 283.

sees the sacrificial and legal images in Scripture as the core foundation for a doctrine of atonement. Calvin insists that the justice that is made ours in justification is an acquired justice that the God-man acquired through the acts of obedience that He performed throughout His life in His divine-human unity. We are made participants in the righteousness of Christ through the work of the Holy Spirit.[15]

Central to Calvin's doctrine of atonement is his understanding of Christ as mediator. He gave new depth to the Reformed doctrine of atonement by introducing the threefold distinction between the offices of Christ as King, Priest and Prophet. Christ's work on the cross is mediatory, that is, He intercedes between God and humankind and reconciles the broken relationship. As King he establishes God's reign on earth and restores the original dominion of humankind, as Priest he represents humanity before God, and as Prophet He reveals God's will to humanity.[16]

Calvin combines the notion of penal satisfaction with the motif of victory. He regards the cross at once as the scene of Satan's definite defeat and the objective basis of justification. Christ conquered sin, death and the devil, yet his victory contains a paradox, because He conquers by being weak.[17] Satan and death draw their power from the administration of divine justice, yet are disarmed by the satisfaction of that justice.[18]

The Reformed Confessions follow Calvin in distinguishing between a twofold satisfaction, namely a satisfaction of the righteous demands of the law and a satisfaction of the penalty due to sin. Article 21 of the Belgic Confession thus states that Christ's death is a payment for our sins, while article 23 affirms that our sins are forgiven because of Christ's obedience, which covers our unrighteousness. The Heidelberg Catechism also asserts in Sunday 6 (answer 17) that Christ came to bear the wrath of God, while Sunday 24 (answer 62) states that God's justice demands full obedience to the law. Unfortunately, the victory motif, which is quite prevalent in the writings of Calvin, is underemphasized in the Reformed Confessions.

15. Cf. McCormack, "For Us and our Salvation," 298.

16. Cf. Calvin, *Inst.* 2.5.1–2.5.6.

17. Ibid., 2.12.2

18. Cf. ibid., 2.12.2 2.16.11, 2.16.15. Blocher, "Atonement in John Calvin's Theology," 290.

Critisism of Satisfaction Theory

The followers of Socinus were the first to launch a criticism of the penal satisfaction theory in the seventeenth century. Since then it has also been severely attacked by, amongst others, enlightenment theologians, liberal Protestant, feminist and postmodern theologians.

The Socinians followed a rationalist method of inquiry that attempted to interpret Christianity in such a way that it would accommodate the views of the Renaissance along with its optimistic view of humanity.[19] They rejected the notion that God needs satisfaction in order to forgive. According to them, whether God forgives or punishes sin does not depend on His nature, but His will. He is, therefore, perfectly able to forgive without demanding satisfaction. To say that God must be satisfied before forgiveness can be possible is to demean His grace and omnipotence. As a matter of fact, the notion of satisfaction is impossible because personal guilt can not be transferred to another person, as is the case with financial debt. To punish one person for the sins of another is cruel and unjust. Even if it were possible for one person's guilt to be transferred to another, it would not be possible for all persons' guilt to be transferred to one individual.[20]

In the nineteenth and early twentieth-century liberal German Protestantism advocated an ethical understanding of the meaning of Christ's death. Albrecht Ritschl (1822–1889) stated that God's reconciliatory work in Christ must not be understood as a judicial act. Notions such as judgement, punishment, satisfaction and compensation belong to the juridical realm, whereas the Christian religion is concerned with the ethical idea of moral guilt.[21] According to Ritschl God is love and his righteousness exists in the fact that He attempts to bring humankind to salvation. However, because of its sin humankind suffers under a sense of guilt and debt. Christ came to free us of this complex of guilt and to obliterate the feeling of mistrust that exists through his faithfulness, which is an expression of Divine love.[22] He does not act as a mediator or substitute, but His work is ethical in nature. Through His passion Christ reveals God's gracious love and imputes His justice to

---

19. Cf. Beeke, "Atonement in Herman Bavinck's Theology," 340.

20. Cf. Bavinck, *Gereformeerde Dogmatiek,* 331.

21. Cf. Ritschl, *Christian Doctrine of Justification and Reconciliation,* 55, 88.

22. Ibid., 53–54, 120.

humankind so that humankind can be taken up in the love of God.[23] Christ's obedience has no effect on God, because God bears no anger that needs to be placated. Neither is Christ's work an attempt to free us from the bondage of Satan. Christ's passion serves us. He attempts to free us from a guilt-ridden consciousness that believes that atonement is only possible through punishment or satisfaction, and to establish a new universal ethical community of humankind that enters into a new relationship with God and a new relationship with the world that is characterised by self-realisation.[24]

Gustav Aulén (1879–1977) published his classical work *Christus Victor* in 1931. In this study Aulén distinguishes among the classic type of atonement, commonly held by the Church Fathers, which states that the essence of Christ's work lies in His victory over the forces of evil, the subjective type, first formulated by Abelard, which views Christ's work as an ethical example of perfect love that serves to extract a responsive love from humanity, and the objective account of atonement first developed by Anselm, that states that God demands satisfaction for the sins that humanity committed. Aulén questions the biblical foundation of the objective view of atonement by stating that the sacrificial images in the New Testament in reality belong to the victory line of thought, not satisfaction. According to Aulén, the essential point in the objective theory is missing in the New Testament's sacrificial imagery, namely the idea that divine justice is aimed at receiving adequate satisfaction for humankind's default condition through the payment made by Christ on its behalf. The New Testament, according to Aulén, understands the sacrifice in a double-sided manner as both an act of God and an act towards God, whereas the objective satisfaction doctrine understands the sacrifice from below as an offering made by humans to God.[25] Aulén claims that the objective idea of atonement gradually rose in a Western Christendom with its typical rationalist Latin understandings of penance, legal relationships and justice. This is totally different from the New Testament setting within which the classical idea of atonement developed.[26] He also questions the objective type's notion that God is

23. Ibid., 71, 446.
24. Ibid., 449, 474; cf. Aulén, *Christus Victor*, 138.
25. Aulén, *Christus Victor*, 72, 77.
26. Ibid., 78, 82.

willing to accept a satisfaction for sins committed, because such a view fails to guard the truth of God's enmity towards sin and weakens God's radical opposition to sin. The notion that Christ's merits can be imputed to human beings is based, according to Aulén, on a materialist view of sin.[27]

At the end of the twentieth century, feminist theology attacked the notion of penal satisfaction with intense rigour. According to them the penal satisfaction theory portrays God the Father as a violent child abuser. They are also critical of the notion of Christ as a universal substitute. Dorothee Sölle presents the most substantial criticism in this regard. According to Sölle a person who acts as a replacement fully takes the place of the one for whose sake the substitution takes place. Such a substitution, though, depersonalises the relationship, because the one who is replaced is treated as if no longer alive. Substitution theory is, according to Sölle, no longer acceptable for the autonomous modern human, because the autonomous decision whereby human beings burden themselves with guilt cannot be undone from outside.[28] The notion that guilt can be transferred to someone else and that someone else can compensate for one's mistakes is false.[29] For Sölle, substitution theory in essence is an insult to human self-awareness. The notion that God's wrath must be satisfied by the sacrifice of Christ before He can show grace has, according to Sölle, no foundation in the New Testament. It is derived from a depiction of God as an antic eastern Despot and leads to an insoluble tension between God's justice and grace.[30] Satisfaction theory limits the spontaneity of God by making Him the object of reconciliation, not the subject. It limits the work of Christ to a mere judicial act and it is exclusive because Christ brings salvation that is totally independent of the human.[31] Christ's representation can, according to Sölle, be only temporary, because the human being is irreplaceable.[32]

Contemporary postmodern theologians follow the broad premises of feminism in dismissing the rationalist epistemology behind

27. Ibid., 92, 147.

28. Cf. Sölle, *Plaatsbekleding*, 17–62.

29. Ibid., 83, 112–13.

30. Ibid., 80, 132–33.

31. Ibid., 80, 132–33.

32. Ibid., 115.

satisfaction theories of the atonement. In their view it reduces otherness by attempting to explain something beyond our conceptual grasp. The radical-orthodox theologian John Milbank, recently attempted to provide a postmodern variation on the classical doctrine of atonement through a metaphorical understanding of Christ's work. He suggests that Jesus's death must not be seen as a redemptive act that brings reconciliation and eternal life, but as a foundational act that allows for new modes of being.[33] The Gospel narratives must be read not as the story of Jesus, but as the story of the foundation of a new city that practises new politics and new forms of communion based on Christ's example of forgiveness.[34] Jesus is simply the founder, the beginning, the first of many.[35] His death is efficacious not because it satisfies God, but because it inaugurates a new political practise of forgiveness, which in itself is continuing atonement.[36] Any cultic understanding of Christ's death is objectionable, because a single death cannot be universally efficacious, nor can a mere belief in the factual event of atonement be uniquely transformative for the individual.[37]

The above mentioned criticisms can, in conclusion, be summarised as follows:

i)   Moral guilt of one person cannot be transferred to someone else.

ii) Cultic understandings of Christ's death depict God as a violent God.

iii) The notion of a single substitute for the sins of many is an affront to individual responsibility.

iv) Penal satisfaction theory uses legal categories to rationalise an event that is essentially ethical in nature and beyond conceptual grasp.

I will now proceed to address these concerns by focussing on the multidimensionality of the biblical images on atonement, the relation be-

---

33. Milbank, "Name of Jesus," 314, 315.
34. Ibid., 317.
35. Ibid.
36. Ibid., 327.
37. Ibid., 315.

tween God and sin, love and justice, and Christ's capacity as both priest and sacrifice.

Understanding Christ's Sacrifice

The Multi-Dimensionality of Biblical Images

The New Testament does not provide a systematic theory of the significance of Christ's death on the cross, but it uses various rich, multifaceted and interrelated images to explain the necessity of Christ's atonement. These images or metaphors point to much more than mere symbolism. They are powerful cognitive instruments that depict reality truly, albeit in an indirect way. In so doing they explain to us the saving significance of Christ's death. The following images can be discerned:

i)   Victory images. The atonement is portrayed as a divine struggle and victory in which Christ triumphs on the cross over the evil powers of this world that hold humanity in spiritual bondage. God reconciles Himself to the whole of the cosmos in Christ. Central texts in this regard are Colossians 2, 1 Cor 15:24, and Phil 2:10, where Christ is portrayed as the Cosmic Redeemer Who conquers the principalities and powers of this world, the miracle narratives in the Gospels where Christ probes the deepest realms of dark demonic powers, and passages in Revelations that depict the defeat of Satan and his expulsion from heaven.[38]

ii) Financial images. The depiction of God's rescue of His people in the language of a financial transaction is very common both in the Old and New Testament. Christ's death is portrayed in the New Testament as a payment for sins that secures the release of the individual sinner, conceived of as a slave, debtor or condemned prisoner.[39] In 2 Pet 2:1 the notion of "buying" is combined with the idea that the believers are now Christ's slaves by virtue of His purchasing them out of their slavery to sin. Often these financial images are used in combination with images derived from other spheres, especially the legal and sacrificial realms.[40]

---

38. Cf. Rev 1:6, 5:10, 12:11, 15:2–3.

39. Cf. 1 Pet 1:18–19, Mark 10:45, Tit 2:14, Rev 1:5, 5:9, Rom 3:9.

40. Cf. 1 Pet 1:18–19, Rev 1:5.

iii) Cultic images. The sacrificial realm accounts for much of the Bible's atonement language. Through his sacrificial death Christ remits the sins of humanity and reconciles human beings with God.[41] Christ is often called the Lamb, the Paschal sacrifice that is slain for the sins of the world and whose blood propitiates the sins of humanity.[42] Other key sacrificial terms that are used are *īlasmos*, *īlasterion* and *katalaggē*. *Īlasmos* denotes the objective means by which sins are forgiven. It expresses the idea that Christ covers sin and takes it away through His sacrifice.[43] According to Kistemaker it can communicate both the sense of propitiation and expiation, and thus express a double meaning, namely to reconcile by appeasing God's anger and to remove sin.[44] *Īlasterion* alludes to the location or place where sins are forgiven. In several places in the New Testament the cross is called *īlasterion*, that is, the place where human beings are delivered from guilt and purified from sin.[45] *Katalaggē* and *katalassein* constitutes the broad framework within which the idea of sacrifice as *īlasmos* and *īlasterion* can arise.[46] It denotes the restoration of original friendly relations. Christ terminates the hostility and estrangement between God and humanity and through this brings reconciliation.[47] Through his sacrifice he renews the covenant between God and human beings and becomes the mediator of a better covenant.[48] The New Testament's depiction of Christ's death as a sacrifice is metaphorical, not in the sense that Christ's death on the cross is unreal, but in the sense that language from the context of the Old Testament is transferred to the New Testament to explain the meaning of Christ's death on the cross. Christ's death cannot be a sacrifice in the cultic sense because He is not sacrificed on an altar by a priest,

---

41. Cf. Rom 3:24–26, Matt 26:28, 1 Cor 15:3, Gal 1:4.

42. Cf. John 1:29, 19:14, 19:29, 19:36, Rev 5:5–6.

43. 1 John 2:2, 4:10; Louw and Nida, *Greek English Lexicon of the New Testament*, 2:504.

44. Kistemaker, "Atonement in Hebrews," 146.

45. Louw and Nida, *Greek English Lexicon of the New Testament*, 2:504.

46. Van Asselt, "Christ's Atonement," 59.

47. Cf. Rom 5:10, 11; Heb 10:28.

48. Hebrews 8.

but it is a sacrifice in the theological sense in that He paid the penalty for the sins of humankind.

iv) Legal images. Whereas the cultic images relate Christ's death on the cross to a sacrifice, legal imagery understands Christ's death in relation to the law of God and the renewal of the covenant. Galatians 3:13, for instance, states that Christ redeemed the faithful from the curse of the law by becoming the cursed in our place. Christ thus not only died for our sins, but actively fulfilled the entire law of God, thereby deserving to be the mediator of the new covenant.[49] At times the legal imagery coincides with sacrificial imagery.

v) Exemplarist images. Exemplarist images are found in the Gospels, Pauline epistles and the epistle of 1 Peter. Jesus' death on the cross is viewed as a demonstration of God's love for humanity. The faithful are called upon to follow the example of Christ in their own lives by imitating him. The Gospels primarily use the word *akoulouthein*, while the Pauline epistles use *mimētēs*. *Akoulouthein* denotes a participation in Christ's legacy through an unconditional obedience to him,[50] while *mimētēs* in a similar fashion alludes to an obedience based on the sacrifice of Christ that is manifested in true discipleship,[51] The intent of these words is not that believers can redeem themselves by following the example of Christ, but that they must partake in his legacy as already redeemed people.

The question is: How should the various images used in the New Testament for the atoning work of Christ be approached? Van Asselt[52] distinguishes between the relativist, pluralist and complementarist theological approaches in history and then endorses a multi-dimensional approach that was first developed by Luco van den Brom. Though Van Asselt primarily refers to the different theological models found in church history, his approach can also be applied to the different images in Scripture.

---

49. Cf. Heb 5:8, 9.
50. Cf. John 12:25, 26, Luke 9:26, Matt 8:22.
51. Cf. 1 Cor 11:1, 1 Tess 1:6, Eph 5:1.
52. Van Asselt, "Christ's Atonement," 63–67.

The relativist model, according to Van Asselt, suggests that the meanings of Christ's death should be located in the cultures in which they were first put forward. It assumes that the truth of a particular model is always contextually determined and that there is no context-independent standard that is universally applicable. The problem with this model, according to Van Asselt, is that a particular model may in fact subvert the context in which it originated. The notion of a sacrifice that sacrifices itself is a good example. The pluralistic view, in contrast, allows the diverse models to stand alongside one another as equally valid theories without making any judgement. Each model is true in its own way. Van Asselt, though, is of the view that possible conflicts between the models cannot be settled with reference to the models themselves. A complementary model entails that the different models supplement each other and together offer the complete picture of the significance of Christ's death. However, the idea of complementarity is problematic because the various images concerning Christ's death interact and interpret each other. Instead, Von Asselt proposes a multi-dimensional approach. All the models together constitute an extended chain or family from which one cannot isolate or eliminate a single model. According to Von Asselt the substitution theory offers many possibilities for integrating the dimensions of other models. When we employ the substitution model to organize or structure our perspective on atonement, the other models fall into place automatically and become visible based on their own, albeit limited, validity. A multi-dimensional approach opens up the possibility of a more encompassing model that includes other minor models that are successful in their own right.

Van Asselt's approach seems to be the most adequate, especially since the New Testament itself uses the various images in an intertwined way. Hebrews 2:14–17 for example mixes the victory motif of the Devil's defeat with the sacrificial image of Christ's priesthood, Col 2:14–15 conjoins the victory motif of Christ's triumph with the image of legal debt, Rom 3:24–26 uses the law-court language of justification and redemption, but also makes sacrificial mention of "blood," and 1 Pet 1:18–19 employs economic images in combination with sacrificial terms. Numerous other texts follow the same technique. The intertwined way in which New Testament texts use these images suggests an underlying doctrinal scheme. The images fittingly complement each other. They exhibit the same structure, so that they naturally translate into one another—hence the intertwining in so many passages.[53] Thus there seems to be no disunity between the key images.

Yet all of the images are not of the same importance. The cultic, victorious and legal images are used most frequently, whereas the financial and exemplarist images are usually mentioned in relation to the other images. The economic, victorious and exemplarist images furthermore lack objective foundation without the added significance of the cultic and legal images. It seems therefore that the different images must be interpreted in terms of each other, and that the cultic and legal images must be regarded as providing the objective foundation of a doctrine of atonement, whereas the economic, victorious and exemplarist images deepen the meaning of Christ's atoning work. The idea of substitution and representation links the different images together.

In my view, the Reformed doctrine of penal substitution with its dependence on the cultic and legal images provides the most extensive and biblically responsible theory on atonement. Yet it also displays an element of one-sidedness, due to its lack of emphasis on the victory motif. Because emphasis is placed on Christ as mediator, the call on the faithful is to trust and believe, whereas the importance for obedience and allegiance to Christ, which is prevalent in the victory motif, is often neglected. The atonement, furthermore, entails more than reconciling the broken relationship between God and human beings. As Aulén[54] rightly indicated, salvation and atonement cannot be separated as two distinct ideas. Atonement between God and the world is only possible because Christ broke the power of evil and death through his victory on the cross.

God and Sin

Christ's death is seen in relation to sin, especially in the Pauline epistles. Sin is inherently a violation of God's self-expressed will and is by nature directed against God's person, which is holy and righteous. According to Paul, the law as the revealed will of God is the criterion for establishing sin.[55] It accuses the human and establishes guilt with an ensuing liability

---

53. Cf. Blocher, "Biblical Metaphors and the Doctrine of the Atonement," 643–44.

54. Cf. Aulén, *Christus Victor*, 71.

55. Cf. Gaffin, "Atonement in the Pauline Corpus," 147. Rom 3:20.

for punishment. The issue of atonement is therefore unavoidably legal and penal. Though God's atoning work must not be exclusively viewed in legal terms, we cannot speak about sin and atonement without using legal categories of thinking. The law is an expression of God's being, and therefore cannot simply be nullified by the free grace of God as the Socinians seem to think. The purely ethical approach that rejects the notion of Christ's death as punishment for our sins is also unacceptable, because it implies that the issue of sin is either irrelevant or not that serious in nature. Ritschl's notion that Christ came to free us from our sense of guilt through his example of love, and Milbank's understanding of the work of Christ as inaugurating a new community based on the principle of forgiveness, both fail to comprehend the serious nature of sin and God's radical hostility to evil. They overemphasize God's love at the expense of God's righteousness, and separate God's reconciliatory acts from His justifying acts by not reflecting sufficiently on the issue of accountability. The existence of sin establishes a need for accountability, for if no person is called to account for his actions, the notion of sin becomes meaningless. If punishment were not necessary, God's will would be arbitrary and inconsistent in nature, because He would possess no need to uphold the law, which is an expression of His will.

The New Testament, in contrast, emphasizes the seriousness of sin. It defines sin not merely as a subjective phenomenon, but also as an objective reality that systemically penetrates God's creation and human nature. Paul emphasizes that sin entails more than a mere personal choice, it is an enslaving power that is systemic in nature and cosmic in range.[56] Sin brings bondage and debt. It causes defilement, incurs legal guilt and deserves the ultimate punishment of death.[57] Since the legal effects of sin are both personal and universal in nature, nothing can escape God's punishment. Christ, therefore, has to act as Substitute, because humankind is not able to compensate for something that is part of its very nature. By doing this Christ voluntarily serves the general benefit of all parties concerned in the covenant.

Sölle's criticism that the idea of a substitute is an insult to human autonomy is not valid, because she displays an idealistic view of freedom as a human characteristic that is universally embedded in the autonomy

56. Romans 3.

57. Cf. Rom 1:32.

of the human being and not dependent on prior historical events. Sin, however, is systemic in nature and its effects cannot be avoided through autonomous decision-making. It is precisely because of the objective systemic nature of sin, that the idea of a universal substitute makes perfect sense.

Love and Justice

No conception of the atonement can escape reflection about the Divine nature. When we speak about God's reconciliatory actions we are after all speaking about the coherence of his attributes, especially the relationship between his love and righteousness. God's omnipotence and sovereignty does not mean that He acts randomly or arbitrarily. God is a law unto Himself, and acts according to His attributes. This does not mean that God is not free, His actions according to His attributes are the expression of the highest form of freedom.

Scripture reflects on God's righteousness within a covenantal rather than merely legal framework. Vanhoozer[58] rightly notes that in the context of God's covenant with Israel, the law served the purpose of regulating relationships, both within the covenant community and between the covenant community and God. From a biblical perspective then, God's justice is a matter of his preserving the right covenantal relationships, and of doing so with integrity as a holy, just and loving God. If God should show love without justice, His holiness would not be served. If He shows justice without compassion, His love is compromised. God therefore can only be true to Himself if He exercises justice in love and love in justice. True justice demands some kind of penalty for the infraction of law. A law that carries no sanctions is a misnomer and has no authority. However, God's justice does not bring annihilation, but, in correspondence with God's loving nature, reconciliation. This becomes evident in the New Testament's claim that Christ did not come to destroy the Law, but to fulfil it.[59] The relation between God's justice and love exists therein that God's love is the motivating cause in His exercise of justice. He judges in order to reconcile. His judgement is an instrument of salvation and falls within the framework of divine compassion. On the other hand, God's love co-exists with His holiness

58. Vanhoozer, "Atonement in Postmodernity," 380–81.

59. Cf. Mat 5:17.

and veracity and is therefore a righteous love that God exercises in a way that is faithful to Himself. A love that ignores wrong is unholy, unjust and not perfect love. The satisfaction of Christ thus displays a twofold direction: it satisfies God's demand for justice, but it also satisfies His love by making redemption possible.

Christ as Priest and Sacrifice

Waltke[60] states that the removal of sins in the Old Testament involves two aspects: the external liturgical sacrifices such as the sin and guilt offerings that through the shedding of blood made payment in expiation for a life which was forfeited, and the internal spiritual factors involved in forgiveness which include the personal willingness of God to forgive sin and the offender's willingness to renounce his wrongdoing. The atonement effected by the sacrifices remained highly restricted. They did not cover the whole of life, nor all types of sin, but served only to arouse a sense of guilt. In fact, some Old Testament passages express an awareness that external offerings are not spiritually adequate and could ultimately not be effectual.[61] Bavinck rightly notes that the ceremonial dispensation in the Old Testament was temporary in nature and that it merely served a symbolic and typical purpose. God used the ceremonies to uphold the redemptive-historical purposes and anticipations of the law.[62]

The New Testament depicts Christ as the fulfilment of the promises and anticipations of the Old Testament. Christ's sacrifice is a sign of God's great love, and also of the reality of God's judgement on sin. He acts as the complete antitype of the old sacrificial order in that He is both subject and object in the outpouring of God's wrath. Christ is subject (priest) in the sense that the punishment for sin is an act of the triune God, He is object (sacrifice) in the sense that he takes the consequences of human sin on himself and thereby substitutes and represents the faithful. As such He is both the expiation that covers sin and the propitiation that turns away God's anger, He is both victor and victim.[63] Christ secures permanent purity, thereby eradicating the ef-

60. Waltke, "Atonement in Psalm 51," 51.

61. Cf. Ps 40:6, Mic 6:6-7, Heb 10:4, Isa 1:11, 12.

62. Bavinck, *Gereformeerde Dogmatiek*, 315. Cf. Carson, "Atonement in Romans 3:21–26," 139.

63. Cf. Heb 2:17, Rom 3:25, 1 John 2:1–2.

fects of sin and making God's judgement of His people obsolete. In doing so, Christ embodies and personalises the old sacrificial order in Himself, but at the same time brings the repetitive old sacrificial order to an end by being the perfect sacrifice that satisfies God's holiness. His shed blood is a sign that God has proved His covenantal faithfulness precisely by undergoing the sanctions, legal and relational, for covenantal disobedience.[64] God in Christ thereby subverts not only the old sacrificial system, but also the legal logic of human law, because God sacrifices God, God placates God, God is both the subject and object of reconciliation, God is both Judge and Advocate.

The question is: is this manner of speaking rationally coherent? Carson[65] importantly notes that a distinction must be made between a human judicial system where the judge is an administrator of a system and thus serves something bigger than himself. In such a system it would be a perversion of justice if the Judge takes the place of the offender, because the judge would act against the laws of the land. Yet when God is Judge, He is never Administrator of a system external to Himself, He is the offended party as well as the impartial Judge. Thus to force the categories of human law on divine realities is bound to lead to distortion. Though God is a righteous Judge, He is not a dispassionate or distanced Judge. Since humanity cannot bear the penalty to the end, he sends a Substitute through whom God simultaneously wipes out the sins of the offenders and keeps His own justice intact. He accomplishes this dual act by making human nature part of his own nature. Christ's conflict and victory is thus the conflict and victory of God Himself.

The notion of Socianism that it would be unfair of God to transfer guilt to an innocent person, and the criticism of feminism that the penal satisfaction theory depicts God as a child abuser Who acts violently towards his own Son is founded on a tritheistic understanding of the operation of the triune God. The ontological premise seems to be that God the Father acts as a separate individual towards His Son, Who is a second distinct individual Who operates apart from the triune divine nature. However, the passion of Christ is a triune event during which the triune God pours His wrath out on Himself in and through His second nature, which He has made His own in His second mode of

---

64. Vanhoozer, "Atonement in Postmodernity," 399.

65. Carson, "Atonement in Romans 3:21–26," 132–33.

being. God the Father is thus not doing something to someone else, but He takes the human experience of forsakenness into His own existence through God the Son by giving Himself to sinners in an act of self-sacrificial love. God is not an angry God from whom forgiveness must be elicited by someone who is able to change his attitude and turn his anger into compassion through a violent death.[66] Forgiveness is rather effected by God the Father through His Son. God first loves us, then He reconciles us. Human beings respond to God's grace through the Spirit and participate through the Spirit in the life of the Trinity. In this way human life conforms to God's own life, without jeopardizing the transcendence of God.

The criticism of postmodernist philosophers that the penal satisfaction theory legitimates a violent circle of retaliation misses the point. God has to deal with the illegality of sin. By taking the human experience into His own existence through Christ He in actual fact ends the cycle of retaliation, and negates the need for judgement on every individual without ignoring the illegality of sin.

But can the the guilt of many be imputed to one innocent individual? The transference of human guilt to Christ must, in my view, be understood from the perspective of the covenant that is eternal, divine and collective in nature and transcends the individualistic characteristics of modern human law. Christ acts as Head of the covenant community who in union with him constitutes one corporate body that is collectively accountable before God.[67] Even though sin did not inhere in the person of Christ, God imputed guilt to Christ because He did not punish a single individual in a subjective sense, but human nature as such, which, because of the objective nature of sin, shares a collective guilt. In his bearing of the punishment for sin, Christ, though sinless, does not act as an innocent human being, but He voluntarily takes it on Himself to represent sinful human nature in a generic sense as the Second Adam who, as God-man, takes the human experience into the life of the triune God Himself in order to restore the integrity of the covenant between God and the faithful. Sölle's view that substitution necessarily entails depersonalisation in actual fact stands in opposition to the biblical notion of substitution that entails precisely the contrary,

66. Cf. Bavinck, *Gereformeerde Dogmatiek*, 353, 384. John 3:16, Rom 5:8, 8:32, 1 John 4:9, 10.

67. Cf. 1 Corinthians 12, Ephesians 4.

namely that the faithful discover their true original identity through the transference of guilt and punishment to their representative Jesus Christ.

Conclusion

The difference between the penal substitutionary doctrine of atonement and other theories of atonement lies in the fact that it provides a Scripture-founded model that succeeds in unifying the different metaphors of Scripture by using the sacrificial and legal images as the objective core. The moral-influence type models that were advanced by different theological traditions throughout history lack an objective foundation because of their denial of the sacrificial and substitutionary nature of Christ's death and the radical consequences of sin. As a result they risk setting the Old Testament and New Testament, law and salvation, justice and love, sin and redemption, against each other as irreconcilable features. The sacrificial and substitutionary feature of Christ's death is both a mystery and gift and therefore falls beyond our conceptual grasp in a certain sense. Yet, Christ's work is not irrational nor inexplicable, but makes sufficient sense if we understand that sin is both a subjective and objective reality, that Christ represents sinful human nature in a generic sense on the cross, that God punishes in order to reconcile, and that Christ is not a third party who placates God's anger, but that He is both priest and sacrifice that takes the human experience into the triune God's existence.

PART TWO

Ethical Perspectives

on Dignity, Equality, and Freedom

5

Human and Non-Human Dignity[1]

Introduction

THE ECOLOGICAL CRISIS WHICH WE ARE CURRENTLY EXPERIENCING IS not just "ecological" in nature, nor can it be solved by purely technical means.[2] It not only demands an energy revolution, but also a moral and legal revolution.

Contemporary liberal human rights discourse seems to be inefficient in the face of the ecological threats that we are facing, because it is so formal in structure, so tilted towards individual entitlements, so engrained in modernity that the definitions of human dignity it issues are not adequate to address the global ecological crisis. Rights can, according to the general legal definition only be attributed to subjects of law who are rational beings that can grasp moral law and act as advocates for their interests. Little opportunity is provided for obligations to anything that is not free and rational.

Modern society requires an ethical and legal discourse that directs itself to the whole of creation, rather than only to human society's dependence on its natural environment or its survival—a discourse that correlates human dignity and ecological justice, human rights and the integrity of nature, and the rights of both present generations and future generations. In order to do this, a conception of dignity is needed that will be able to relate human and non-human dignity. Biblical literature and Christian ethics may be helpful in this endeavour because they pose no either/or choice between caring for people and caring for the

1. This chapter was originally published as "Relating Human and Non-human Dignity," *Scriptura* 2.104 (2010) 406–16. Permission has been granted by the editor.

2. Moltmann, *Creating a Just Future*, 53.

earth,[3] yet they give dignity a multi-relational content and are focused on the well-being of the whole.

The aim of this chapter is to offer a definition of dignity that might help to relate human and non-human dignity to each other.

A Theological Perspective on Human and Non-Human Dignity

Modern environmental ethics holds different views on the question of whether nature has intrinsic value. The anthropocentric tradition maintains that only conscious agents possess an intrinsic value. Nature has value insofar as it is useful to human beings. The non-anthropocentric tradition argues that nature is valuable apart from its usefulness to humans.

Through the ages the Christian tradition was largely influenced by the anthropocentric tradition. Christian theology has tended to over-emphasise human history at the expense of natural history, the transcendence of God at the expense of the immanence of God, and human salvation to the detriment of cosmic salvation. Certain strains of Christian theology developed a dualistic eschatology and anthropology which devalued the material world and the bodily realm. Spiritualist and ascetic Christian movements often proclaimed the cosmic homelessness of the human being thereby alienating humans from their environment, whereas some theologians gave modernistic interpretations of the cultural mandate found in Genesis 1 which exhibited confidence in unfailing technological and social progress. Yet the Bible itself, in my view, is not responsible for the ecological-crisis, but on the contrary, rather holds promise to address the ecological crisis which we are currently experiencing. The main themes in the Bible provide Christians with creative tools to address the ecological crisis and to resolve the tensions between human and non-human dignity.

The Divine Origin and Interrelatedness of All Things

In the creation narratives human beings as well as the natural environment derive their dignity from God Who is the Origin and Sustainer of all life. God brought life into a state of total inhabitability by separating

---

3. Cf. Hessel, "Eco Justice after Nature's Revolt," 11.

the chaotic and unfriendly elements from the friendly elements to create an environment in which humans and nature can live in peace and harmony.

The life-giving breath of God is the vital principle of life. In the Jahwist creation narrative humans receive life through a special act of God. God animates the human body with His divine breath. This serves as an affirmation of the ontological and sacred status of human life. The human being only comes to life because God breathes into him His own breath of life. When God withdraws His breath of life, everything returns to dust. The animal kingdom is also called into existence by divine breath, but only in the case of the human being is reference made to a direct transfer of the divine breath. Yet, the whole world is dependent on God, constantly depending on His breath of life to go forth to renew the created order.

The transcendence of God must therefore not be emphasized at the expense of God's immanence. Creation has dignity because God dwells in it through His Spirit and sustains it. The special dignity of Creation lies in the fact that each living creature has been willed into existence by God and has an immanent quality bestowed by Him.[4] *Immanent quality* means that living organisms achieve vitality when they serve the functions and ends that God assigns them. All organisms play their part in the complex of habitat. In the Priestly creation narrative emphasis falls on the fact that God created plants, trees and animals each according to its own *kind*. All things therefore received some unique quality that man must respect in his dominionship, because creation is an ordered totality that comprises a complex variety.

According to the Priestly creation narrative human beings were created on the same day as the animals. Both proceed from the earth and in their nature and existence belong to it. This is an important testimony to the intimate relation between human and non-human creatures. The narrators show thereby that animals and humans belong together and share a common environment and living space. The older Jahwist account presents the same view by emphasizing that human beings are, like animals, *living creatures*. The human environment is immersed in the natural environment.

---

4. Cf. Vischer, "Listening to Creation Moaning," 23.

Everything exists, according to the creation narratives, through God and in God. The Spirit of God is present everywhere and sustains, nourishes and gives life to all things in heaven and on earth. God reveals Himself in the structure of the world and has imprinted in His individual works marks of His glory. Nature has an inherent dignity because it mediates awareness of the divine.

The divine origin and interrelatedness of all things underlies the biblical concept of the human being. The Priestly narrative describes the human being as created in the image of God. Chapter 1 discussed the interpretational difficulties with regard to the meaning of the *imago Dei* at length. It will suffice at this point to reiterate that Gen 1:26–28 gives a cautious and open-ended account of the meaning of the human being's image in relation to God. Through the interchangeable use of *děmût* and *ṣelem* it attempts to relate the human being to God, but at the same time it also emphasizes the innate difference between God and the human being. The human being's image contains both a relational element and a hierarchical and biological component. It signifies the relation between God, the human being and creation, yet these relationships are also hierarchical in nature.

The *Imago Dei* firstly refers to the capability of the human being to have a relationship with God, fellow-human beings and the natural environment. It emphasizes that human beings are God's representatives on earth and are endowed with a special dignified status. The dignity of humankind is not based on something intrinsic to its nature, but lies in its relation to God. The image of God is only applied to humans, never to animals. This is of crucial importance in understanding what makes humans different from animals. The human creature is called to enter into a conscious communion with God, while there is no such relationship between God and the non-human realm. The human's image of God refers to those special dimensions of human nature that elevate humans above the animal plane, such as personhood, self-awareness and self-determination.[5] Human beings are thus unique among God's creatures, but they also form part of the entirety of creation.

The human being's createdness as male and female is closely related to his or her relationship with God. In the same way that God has the ability to deliberate with Himself, that is, to be singular, yet at

---

5. Cf. Anderson, *From Creation to New Creation*, 12.

the same time plural, the human being is created singular, as a human being that shares a common humanity, but also plural as male and female, who are sexually differentiated. Likeness to God cannot be lived in isolation. The human being is created as a social being. Interhuman communication, forming relationships, the ability to love, associate and express emotions and ideas are all reflections of the virtues of God Himself. The deliberative quality of God, which is transferred to human beings, allows people to deliberate about the usefulness of other species in relation to human ends, but this must be done in a way that respects God and the well-being of His creation.

Though personhood, self-awareness and self-determination are also considered as important in liberal human rights discourse, there is a distinct difference between the Christian and liberal philosophical understanding of these human attributes and their ethical application. In liberal rights discourse personhood, self-awareness and self-determination are grounded in the autonomous nature of the rational human being and are, therefore, understood in an anthropocentric sense as qualities that give humans the right to be free of external constraint. In biblical literature personhood, self-awareness and self-determination have a theocentric origin and are inextricably linked to humans' ability and responsibility to respond to God and their environment. These are created attributes that the human needs in order to relate to God and the environment, and they serve the function of engagement, not disengagement.

Secondly, the *Imago Dei* possesses a biological and hiërarcial component. Genesis 1:28 charges human beings to exercise dominion over the non-human realm as God's representatives on earth. Though the Hebrew verbs used in Gen 1:26–28 for *dominion* have a violent meaning in other contexts[6], they are used within the Priestly account in the context of harmony. As stated in chapter1, the intention of Gen 1:26–28 is that humans must exercise their dominion over the earth within limits, that is, in responsibility to the Creator and in a way that will enhance the Creator's earth and all its creatures.[7] This is affirmed in Gen 2:15 where the humans' responsibility towards creation is depicted as *taking*

---

6. Cf. Joel 3:13, Jer 34:15.

7. Cf. Bruegemann, *Theology of the Old Testament*, 461.

care. Passages in the Pentateuch also contain various laws aimed at the protection of the environment.[8]

From the abovementioned it becomes clear that the value of the relationship between human beings and the non-human realm lies in its relatedness to God. Moltmann[9] rightly states with regard to human dignity the following:

> The dignity of human beings is unforfeitable, irrelinguishable and indestructible, thanks to the abiding presence of God.

Dignity is a multi-relational term. Here the Judeo-Christian tradition and the classic-liberal tradition part ways. The Enlightenment based human dignity in intrinsic qualities of the human, such as rationality, with the result that dignity received a foundation in the bearer himself. The weakness of this tradition is that it tends to overemphasise the autonomy and independence of the individual at the expense of the social and natural dimensions of human life. This happens because this line of thought seeks to preserve human dignity by protecting the independence of the human being, without sufficiently realising the importance of relationships for human dignity. The Biblical tradition, in contrast, shows that human dignity is bestowed by God within a specific relational structure. Human dignity therefore has two main features: Firstly it is inviolable because it is God-given. Every human being is entitled to respect. This implies that state authorities have to respect this entitlement in itself and to protect it where it is threatened or disregarded.[10] It also implies that human beings have a fundamental right to self-determination and self-realisation. Secondly, human dignity is an ethical category that involves rights but also duties, because the human being is an individual in communion with fellow human beings and the environment. The Christian faith never sees the individual as the mere bearer of interests and intentions, but always as part of an interwoven structure of relationships and responsibilities, regardless of whether the individual is aware of this structure or not.[11] Future rights discourse will have to place more emphasis on duties, especially on the duties of

---

8. Exod 23:10–12, Lev 26:34, Deut 20:15, 19–20, 22:6, 25:4.

9. Moltmann, *God in Creation*, 233.

10. Vogel et al., *Human Dignity*, 20.

11. Ibid., 28.

humans towards the environment, in order to address the ecological crisis.

Since the human being's dignity is exercised within a God-given relational structure, the state needs to protect the relational structure itself into which the human being is born. The social dimensions of human relationships, as well as the relationship between the human being and the natural environment, must be guarded because the human being is dependent upon these relationships. Humans therefore have a right to development such as exercising culture, having children, forming families and having education. They also have environmental rights such as access to food, water, and a clean and healthy environment. If the state does not protect the relational structure into which human beings are born, individual dignity will ultimately vanish because dignity can't survive if the God-given relational structure is annihilated.

Sin and the Covenant

Genesis 1:26 defines the appropriate nature of humanity in the world, whereas the rest of the primeval narrative demonstrates the human being's misuse of the rule that the image of God conferred on him. In the narrative of the Garden of Eden the human couple rebels against God by trying to be like Him. This disrupts their relationship with God, each other, non-human creation and the soil on which they depend for their existence. The relational structure that God created has become distorted. Humankind's sin leads to a return to chaos. In the Priestly narrative the flood is portrayed as a return to the initial watery chaos that characterised the uncreated world.

God makes a new beginning with humankind by entering into covenantal relationships with His people. The history from creation to Exodus-Sinai is divided into a sequence of covenants, each of which is declared an everlasting covenant. The first period extends from creation to the Flood and is concluded by a covenant between God and Noah. This covenant is not only universal in that it embraces all peoples, but it is also an ecological covenant that includes the earth itself and all of its inhabitants. It reaffirms the creational doctrine that God is committed to the preservation of creation. Because God commits Himself to creation, humans will fulfil their destiny by also committing themselves to the created world. While God makes a covenant with all living human beings in Genesis 9, human beings and animals are not assigned the same value. Human beings may not kill each other, but God gives them permission to eat animals. Though the ecological covenant affirms the intrinsic value of all creatures, it does not mean that all beings have the same status before God.[12]

Both the Abrahamitic and Sinaitic covenants contain a strong ecological motive. They emphasise the importance of land as a gift of God. The gift of land is seen in the Old Testament as an expression of God's covenantal love and faithfulness. Many texts in the Old Testament reflect the close relationship between the people and the soil. Land is treated as part of the covenantal community: If the people obey God the land will flourish, but when the Israelites spurn the worship of JHWE and neglect the demands of divine justice, the effects also impact on the land. The importance of land for human welfare is furthermore clearly illustrated in passages of the Torah, which contain environmental laws that are aimed at protecting the land.[13] These commands flow from the sense of covenant community and respect for each other as beings in the image of God.

The Sinaitic covenant proclaims a strong Sabbath ethic that is also applied to the land. The aim of the Sabbath ethic is to protect the created relational structure. Human intervention with nature ought to cease for the duration of the Sabbath. In the seventh year Israel has to leave the land untouched. The goal is twofold: the poor have to be provided the opportunity to assemble food from the lands and the land itself has to rest. In Leviticus 25 the commandment contains a warning: If the people do not obey the rule of the Sabbath year, God will exile the people from His land so that the land can recover and celebrate its Sabbath with God. In this case, the integrity of the land is considered more important than the rights of the peoples. The decline of the ecology is seen as a result of human injustice.

Future generations also share in the created relational structure. Every covenant in Scripture assumes responsibilities towards future generations, because the covenants are made "with you and your offspring" forever.[14] This refrain frequently recurs in the Old Testament

12. Cf. Cobb, "Postmodern Christianity in Quest of Eco-Justice," 33.

13. Cf. Exod 23:12, Lev 25:4–8, Exod 23:10.

14. Gen 3:15. Nash, *Loving Nature*, 101.

and establishes a trans-generational continuity, a set of obligations that link past, present and future.

The Cosmic Dimension of Redemption

Traditional theology often emphasised the personal dimension of God's redemption at the expense of the cosmic dimension by focussing exclusively on God's history with humanity, whereas the natural world was regarded as a stage for the divine-human drama.[15]

However, the cosmic dimension of God's redemptive work is affirmed both in Old and New Testament literature. Old Testament prophetic-eschatological literature expresses it through the word *shalom*.[16] God will create a condition of peace on earth by transforming people, relations between Israel and the nations, and nature itself. In Deutero-Isaiah the universal liberation that God brings is founded in the concept that God is not only the Redeemer of Israel, but also the Creator of heaven and earth.[17] The non-human realm will, therefore, also share in God's eschatological promises.

The New Testament portrays Christ as not only the Saviour of humankind, but also the cosmos. His incarnation confers dignity not only on humankind, but on all earthly and material things, because by becoming flesh Christ indicates that the material world is part of His salvational work. According to the Gospels Christ is the mediator of creation Who brings God's Kingdom to earth.[18] God's Kingdom is portrayed as a future reality that is also a present reality, since the revelation of Christ is the revelation of the Kingdom. Christ's rule over all things has already started and has cosmic implications for the present. Christians, therefore, cannot abandon this earth, because Christ came to renew this earth as our final destination.

In Pauline literature the final fulfilment has an integrative function in the sense that the whole of creation is destined for redemption and included in God's final aim. In Col 1:20 and Eph 1:10 Christ is depicted as the Firstborn of all creation and the Reconciler that holds all things together. Christ is the Foundation of all things, reconciling all things in

15. Santmire, "Healing the Protestant Mind," 57.

16. Isa 11:1–9, Ezekiel 34.

17. Isa 42:5, 44:25.

18. Cf. John 1:1–3, Matt 4:17.

heaven and on earth with God. He died not only for humankind, but all beings. By conquering sin He restores human relationships with God and with nature and salvages the relational structure of creation as a whole.

Since God is the Origin of all things and all things are interrelated, God's salvation will not be fully accomplished if His redemptive work does not extend to the whole of creation. As long as creation is unredeemed, Christians will suffer affliction. In Romans 8 the destiny of creation is bound to the destiny of humanity. The whole of creation is portrayed as groaning in travail, awaiting liberation from futility and decay. It expects redemption from the powers of sin and death which have already been experienced by believers who received the first fruits of the Spirit. This does not mean that all creatures will partake in the same glory as the children of God, but that they will share in the better state in their own way.

Romans 8 portrays God as immanently involved in creation through His Spirit, though still distinct from it. The Spirit leads Creation to its purpose, namely its redemption and perfection, with the result that creation becomes an instalment of the future and the embodiment of promise. An eschatology that takes into account the cosmic dimension of God's redemptive work and God's immanent involvement in creation can never support the notion that the cosmos is not really our home. It will always create cosmic optimism since earthly existence is meaningful, not pointless.

Translating Christian Principles to the Public Realm

The current ecological crisis is of such magnitude that the mere propagation of a new lifestyle will not suffice. Political and legal reform are needed to establish legal rules for relationships to muster sufficient power in order to address the current scale of the ecological crisis. Stephen Toulmin[19] rightly states that instead of viewing the world of nature as onlookers from outside, we now have to understand how our human life and activities operate as elements within the world of nature. Political and legal reform is needed to establish legal rules for relationships that will muster sufficient power to address the current scale of the ecological crisis. Human rights discourse will have to accept

19. Toulmin, *Return to Cosmology*, 255.

that human beings are not masters of the environment, but participants in the eco-system and that human justice depends on ecological justice. It will have to address the inherent conflicts between the interests of present generations and those of the future, between human well-being and the protection of nature, and between local and global concerns.

The much debated question of whether an environmental ethic should be based on human needs or upon nature itself is a false question. Human needs and the integrity of nature are interdependent. It therefore seems as if the human rights discourse will have to part ways with the Kantian grounding of rights and intrinsic value in the autonomy and rational consciousness of human beings. Though human consciousness is a source of values, it does not mean that it is the locus of value.[20] Human needs and the integrity of nature are interdependent. Rights need to be defined multi-relationally in the light of the relational structure of which human beings are the most important part. The value of human beings lies in their relatedness to God. This presupposes certain inviolable entitlements and correlating duties. Human beings are, however, also participants in a divinely created relational structure whose maintenance is a prerequisite for the realisation of human dignity. Humans therefore have natural rights to use natural resources to satisfy human needs, but also the moral responsibility to safeguard the relational structure that God created. This entails that humans must care for and nurture the natural environment.

The definition of human dignity as a multi-relational term might help to resolve the impasse between the anthropocentric and non-anthropocentric tradition in environmental ethics. Gustafson[21] states an important ethical principle in this regard:

> Nature is a multidimensional source of values, and its values are specified in relation to other things, other values that we cherish.

In other words, the value of nature's parts are measured in relation to other parts of nature, as well as in relation to the values that human beings cherish as a result of their deliberation. The well-being of the entirety is ultimately a prerequisite for the realisation of individual liberties.

20. Cf. Rolston, "Naturalising Values," 110.
21. Gustafson, *Sense of the Divine*, 113.

If the rights of human beings and the integrity of the environment are not continuously balanced, human development will become unsustainable. However, two fundamental issues need to be addressed: How should people accord dignity to non-human species? How might a revised framework of human rights grant nature's creatures due respect?

How to Grant Dignity to Non-Human Species

The non-anthropocentric notion of "rights of nature" creates many moral and juridical difficulties. From a moral perspective it is clear that nature and animals cannot be granted the same rights as humans. If they were, human civilisation itself would become impossible. Biotic egalitarianism is simply not tenable because we can't do away with the food chain. The recognition of non-human rights will, furthermore, make judicial adjudication extremely difficult and complex, because it is not easy to define the scope and content of such rights.

The anthropocentric notion of human dignity that bases rights in the autonomous rational nature of humans is also insufficient, because it tends to reduce nature to a mere means, while human beings are the measure of all things. Anthropocentric values are of crucial importance as far as environmental policy is concerned, yet it is dangerous to limit our defence of nature to arguments based on its usefulness to us.[22]

A third paradigm, that is neither anthropocentric nor non-anthropocentric, is needed in judging nature's value. The definition of dignity as a multi-relational term might help to resolve the abovementioned impasse. This would entail distinguishing between the dignity of the entirety, and human dignity and non-human dignity, that correlates with the dignity of the entirety. Dignity of the entirety entails that the cosmos has a multi-relational structure and that the value of nature's parts are known in relation to other parts of nature and according to the values that human beings cherish.

Human dignity ought to correlate with the dignity of the entirety, because the maintenance of the created relational structure is a prerequisite for the realisation of human dignity. Humans have natural rights to utilise natural resources to satisfy human needs, but also the moral responsibility to safeguard the relational structure created by God. Human dignity consists in a person's right to personhood, self-

22. Cf. Hettinger, "Comments on Holmes Rolston's Naturalizing Values," 122.

awareness and self-determination as well as his right to have access to the basic conditions that are required to fulfil his role as caretaker of God's created order and to live a meaningful life in harmony with God and nature. Such basic conditions include the right to life, physical security, a clean environment and freedom. Personhood, self-awareness and self-determination are not goals in themselves but are created attributes that enable man to serve the needs of other creatures and to enhance the health of the entirety of creation. Freedom must be constrained when an individual exercises these attributes in such a way that he affects the well-being of the entirety.

Non-human dignity is determined by the role which a part of nature plays in the whole complex of relationships in the created order. A distinction needs to be made between inherent value and rights. Animals and plants are inherently valuable because God created them with immanent qualities, yet they are not the sort of things that can have moral rights, because they cannot reciprocate. This does not mean that humans have no duties towards the non-human realm. Nature cannot reciprocate, but it displays what is to be evaluated. Though we cannot bestow rights on individual animals and plants, human beings have the duty to protect the interdependent relational structure created by God, through assessing the value of a part of nature in relation to the whole interdependent structure of the cosmos. Interventions in nature must therefore always be morally and rationally justified, and proportional in the sense that the minimum intervention must be used to reach the goals envisaged.

The most important element in protecting the relational structure of creation is to protect life itself. The eating of domesticated animals such as sheep, or experiments on mice, for instance, are morally justified as long as they are not cruel, because they will not harm the well-being of the entirety, but the destruction of species and eco-systems needs extraordinary moral justification, since it jeopardises the well-being of the entirety. When species are destroyed, the vitality of life itself is destroyed, since lost species can never be reproduced. Even "bad kinds" of species play useful roles in population control, in symbiotic relationships, or in providing opportunities for other species.[23] Ecosystems are important because they are fundamental units of survival that generate

23. Rolston, "Environmental Ethics," 81.

and support life, keep selection pressures high, enrich situated fitness, and allow congruent kinds to evolve in their places with sufficient containment. Since ecosystems are selective systems that increase kinds of life, they can never be regarded as merely nominal. They are integral to the created relational structure.

Though the codification of biotic or non-human rights are not legally tenable, environmental interests can be protected through a combination of environmental laws and the recognition of environmental human rights. Environmental laws must protect non-human species and the conditions necessary for their continued existence and ought to provide the basic criteria for making value judgements that determine the role of nature's part in the entirety. Such laws must become part of international law in order to confront the global ecological crisis. Issues that need to be addressed by environmental laws are: sustainable production, the limitation of pollution to levels that do not exceed the absorption capacities of ecological processes, full public disclosure by governments and private enterprises of the practises followed, as well as the risks involved in toxic waste disposal, the equitable sharing of natural resources, the preservation of biodiversity, redress to victims for violations of their environmental rights and the maintenance of ecosystems and related ecological processes essential for the biosphere. Environmental human rights ought to protect the basic conditions needed by humans to fulfil their role and exist within the complex relational structure of the entirety. They entail, inter alia, the right of humans to be able to fulfil their roles as caretakers of creation, have access to clean air, water and food, and to live in a healthy environment and in harmony with existing ecosystems.

Revising the Framework of Human Rights

Since the concepts of human and non-human dignity have to correlate with the dignity of the entirety, a change in the hierarchy of human rights discourse is needed. Human autonomy cannot be protected if basic conditions for a dignified life are not provided. These can in turn not be provided if the relational structure within which human beings function is not protected.

Although first generation rights have traditionally enjoyed preference above second and third generation rights, it is logical that certain key second and third generation rights should enjoy precedence above some first generation rights, because urgent needs are more immediate necessities than higher goods. Typical first generation rights, such as the right to free trade, freedom of movement, the freedom to practise a profession of your choice, the freedom to possess private property, might in future have to be limited in order to protect third generation rights. Such limitations of first generation rights are not only necessary for the environment, but also for economic development as such, because unsustainable economies that damage the environment cannot flourish for long.

A recognition of the rights of future generations is also essential, because a consciousness of our inter-generational responsibilities will awaken a desire to save the world for the countless generations of living beings that should come after us. Theologically speaking, the rights of future generations follow from God's covenant with us and our descendants. In the eyes of God the Creator we and our descendants are partners in the same covenant. Juridically speaking, future generations are members of our moral community because our social ideal is relevant to them.[24]

Future generations need to enjoy rights of status and not only rights of recognition, because their existence can be reasonably anticipated. The historical continuous nature of communities and the high probability of the existence of future generations is sufficient ground for affirming rights and responsibilities. Future generations can be said to have anticipatory and presumptive rights, and every present generation therefore has anticipatory obligations. Responsibilities extend not only in space but in time, in a chain of obligation that is passed from one generation to the other. Obligations to future generations involve producing a desirable state of affairs and promoting good living conditions. Future generation rights would include the right to life, the right not to suffer excessive debts of past generations and the right not to be subjected to the ecological legacy of pollution and environmental degradation. To protect the rights of future generations development needs to be sustainable. Justice demands that economies should be arranged in a way that ensures efficiency and the anticipated participation

24. Cf. Golding, "Limited Obligations to Future Generations," 361.

of future generations. Growth without limits can no longer be defined as healthy economics.

Care for the environment is probably the most profound obligation that present generations have with regard to future generations, because we thereby promote conditions of good living for the community of the future.

Such environmental obligations might include preventing pollution and ecological degradation, promoting conservation, ensuring ecologically sustainable development and a sustainable use of natural resources, while promoting justifiable economic and social development, prohibiting practises such as nuclear proliferation that could jeopardise the opportunities for future generations to come into being, and avoiding ecologically irreversible actions that might endanger future generations or deprive them irreversibly for the sake of present generations.

The legal recognition of the abovementioned rights are tenable, because they are definable, measurable and enforceable. Obviously these rights will have to be balanced with other rights, and might also be limited at times, as is the case in all human rights jurisprudence.

Conclusion

Contemporary human rights discourse over-emphasises the autonomy of the human being at the expense of the relational structure within which human life is embedded. Though it is important to protect the inviolable autonomy of human beings, a multi-relational understanding of dignity that relates human and non-human dignity to the dignity of the entirety is needed. Human beings are participants in a creational structure whose maintenance is a prerequisite for the protection of individual liberties. The value of non-human entities is determined by their role in the entirety of this created order. In future, human rights jurisprudence will have to balance conflicting rights in terms of the well-being of the entirety. This entails that some third generation rights might need to enjoy precedence over certain first generation rights. It is also important that the rights of future generations should be protected in order to prevent inter-generational apathy that leads to environmental degradation.

6

Freedom and Equality[1]

Introduction

FREEDOM AND EQUALITY ARE OFTEN CONSIDERED NATURAL ENEMIES, because it is difficult to balance their conflicting interests and fit them both into a common political system. The main point of disagreement between libertarians and equalitarians concerns the meaning and scope of liberty and equality. The key question is: Does a sound moral justification for positive legal entitlements to goods and services exist, or would the enforcement of positive rights infringe on individual liberty to an unacceptable extent?[2]

Conflict between freedom and equality is especially evident in the economic sphere. In capitalist economies that allow citizens the freedom to dispose of their wealth in a manner they think fit, distributions are often extremely inequalitarian. Equalitarian economies, on the other hand, frequently degenerate into oppression or into the equal distribution of poverty. Communism has demonstrated that legal enforcement of equalitarianism can destroy freedom and liberty, whereas extreme forms of socialism often impoverish societies by compensating people whose rights have not been infringed upon, thereby emphasising collective responsibility for welfare at the expense of personal responsibility.

Social and legal spheres of societies are also characterised by frequent conflict between freedom and equality. In recent years there

1. This chapter was originally published as "Are Freedom and Equality Natural Enemies? A Christian-Theological Perspective," *Heythrop Journal* 51 (2010) 594–609. Used by permission.

2. Buchanan, "Matrix of Contractarian Justice," 81.

has been growing awareness that people are born into different social positions and have different expectations of life, partly determined by the political system and social and economic conditions.[3] Certain individuals cannot compete with others on an equal footing because of historical patterns of discrimination on the basis of gender and race. Many states address this issue by implementing affirmative action policies, taking positive steps in order to eradicate institutionalised inequalities in society.[4] In the process reversed forms of discrimination are legally enforced, which creates difficult legal problems. Some questions that arise are: Should equality enjoy precedence over freedom? Can any form of discrimination ever be justified? Which criteria should be used to distinguish between fair and unfair discrimination? Which freedoms may be restricted and which are inviolable?

The aim of this chapter is to provide a Christian perspective that might help to reconcile conflicts such as these. However, a fundamental question needs to be addressed first: Are religious ethics relevant in discussions on social justice? The first section of this chapter will address this issue by focusing on the Rawlsian concept of overlapping consensus. The second section provides a theological-conceptual framework that might help to resolve conflicts between freedom and equality, and the final section offers a societal framework within which freedom and equality can function as complementing values.

The Need for an Overlapping Consensus

In his famous work, A Theory on Justice, John Rawls argued that a well-ordered society is stable when it is relatively homogeneous in its basic moral beliefs.[5] Applying his hypothesis soon became problematical, because modern democratic societies are characterised by a multitude of incompatible and irreconcilable doctrines that are religious, philosophical and moral in nature.

The question that arose was: How can a plurality of incompatible but reasonable doctrines coexist within the framework of democratic institutions? Rawls addressed this issue in later works by creating the idea of an *overlapping consensus*. According to him a well-ordered

3. Cf. Rawls, *Theory of Justice*, 7.

4. Some recent examples are the United States, Britain, South Africa, and Malaysia.

5. Cf. Rawls, *Theory of Justice*, 397.

society needs an overlapping consensus that allows for a plurality of reasonable, though opposing, comprehensive doctrines, each with its own conceptions of the good. A well-ordered society can be stable when a political concept of justice can be offered that every supporter of a reasonable doctrine can endorse from his or her own philosophical point of view.[6] Such an overlapping consensus is possible, because the history of religion and philosophy shows that there are many reasonable ways in which the wider realm of values can be understood so as to be congruent with, or supportive of, or at least not be in conflict with, the values of the political domain as specified in a political conception of justice.

Rawls' approach is a welcome corrective to the traditional liberal view that only the liberal conception of the common good, based on autonomous reason can be universally recognised in the public domain by all reasonable and rational citizens. The result of this narrow-minded approach was that religious ethics were relegated to the private sphere of life, because they were deemed not applicable to, or not universally acceptable within, the public domain of society. The privatisation of religion suppressed awareness of the inevitable religious foundation of social life and impoverished the public domain, since some public values became ambivalent and opaque because of the loss of people's religious roots.[7]

The traditional liberal approach is increasingly leading to conflict within a rapidly pluralizing world because the liberal cultural force is anything but neutral. Various religious groups view this approach as profoundly threatening because it forces secularism on society, over-emphasizes individual rights at the expense of social responsibility and deforms social institutions and traditions because of its individualistic tendencies. It also lacks integrity, because there is no such thing as law and ethics based upon reason alone. All forms of law and ethics are pre-determined by a basic worldview, which, if not grounded in theology, at least has a theological dimension. Reason cannot be severed from the worldview in which it is grounded. Every worldview is grounded in a specific anthropology, an ethical determination as to what man intends to be and what he regards as the purpose of his existence.

6. Rawls, *Political Liberalism*, 134.
7. Cf. Pannenberg, *Human Nature*, 18.

Recognising the value of religious ethical discourse in formulating views on social justice does not mean that religious people have the right to impose theocratic values upon society. The social union of plural and heterogeneous societies cannot be founded on a common religious faith or philosophical doctrine, but rather on a shared public conception of justice.[8] According to Rawls an overlapping consensus must have three main features. First it must be a consensus of reasonable, as opposed to unreasonable or irrational comprehensive doctrines. Secondly, the consensus must be political in nature and cannot impose religious, metaphysical or epistemological doctrines on society. Thirdly, the consensus must be durable to ensure stability. To attain this groups must not put forward more of their comprehensive views than what is useful for the political aim of consensus.[9]

Christianity has a major public role to play in the search for an overlapping consensus in society. The distinctive contribution of the Christian religion, in contrast to secular morality, is that it brings the whole of reality and existence into some system of coherence.[10] Though Christian morality is primarily intended for Christians, non-Christians can benefit from the insights of Christians. As a matter of fact, the juridical institutions of Western culture are deeply influenced by Christianity. Christianity still forms the moral and philosophical roots of Western culture and has contributed in a fundamental way to the development of the idea of the eternal value of the individual and his life.[11]

Christian ethical views on social justice can operate in an overlapping social consensus under two conditions. Firstly, they must be universally applicable. Christian ethical principles must be translated into language that secular people can understand and apply, without their having to accept the metaphysical doctrines of the Christian faith. This does not mean that the metaphysical doctrines of Christianity are not considered to be true, but simply that the truth of such claims is not at stake here. Secondly, a distinction must be made between theological perspectives that are applicable to the modern political environment and those that are not. Not all biblical perspectives on social justice are

8. Cf. Rawls, *Political Liberalism*, 304.

9. Ibid., 144–48.

10. Cf. Niebuhr, *Interpretation of Christian Ethics*, 15–16.

11. Cf. Pannenberg, *Human Nature*, 14.

applicable to modern society. The egalitarian notions of the deuterono-mistic tradition, for instance, provided for periodic returns to the original social position and cannot be imposed upon modern democratic states with free economies. Such a demand would not be reasonable nor faithful to the biblical message, since the Bible does not attempt to provide a practical model for the organisation of the state, which is applicable to all societies at all times.

A Theological-Conceptual Framework for Resolving the Conflict between Freedom and Equality

Dworkin[12] rightly states that there are different interpretations and conceptions of freedom and equality. Whether we consider freedom and equality to be conflicting ideals will depend on the conceptions of each we adopt.

In the following section I shall attempt to provide a conceptual framework for freedom and equality based on theological perspectives that might help to resolve conflicts between freedom and equality. I will make use of central themes in Scripture such as the *imago Dei*, social justice, the covenant, and the kingdom of God. These themes appear repeatedly in different contexts within Scripture. Scripture also awards them specific theological meaning by relating them to Christ in one way or the other.

A Theological Perspective on Freedom

Although explicit references to the human being as the image of God are found in the Old Testament only in priestly material,[13] it is of enormous importance for the biblical understanding of humanity. The *Imago Dei* is an expression of that which is most distinctive in the human being and his relation to God, namely, that the human is created in the divine image.[14] We can, therefore, never speak about humans in isolation from God. The *Imago Dei* also underlies the concept of the covenant, since it tells us that the human was created by God as a partner capable of entering into a covenantal relationship with God. As noted in chapter

12. Dworkin, *Sovereign Virtue*, 126.

13. Gen 1:26–27; 5:1; 9:6.

14. Cf. Berkhof, *Systematic Theology*, 206. Harland, *Value of Human Life*, 208.

1, the importance of the *Imago Dei* concept is illustrated by the fact that the New Testament expands this concept, giving it a Christological content. Christ is seen as the perfect image of God and as the destiny of humankind.[15] Christians are expected to conform to the image of Christ by following Him.[16]

The *Imago Dei* concept clearly implies that freedom forms part of the structural essence of the human being, who was created by God as a free agent with a free will who is able to choose, act, multiply, labour and cultivate.[17] Freedom, therefore, is an essential feature of a just society. The human's innate freedom is, however, not an invitation to licence and anarchy, because these do not constitute true freedom but enslave people. This is clearly illustrated in the Jahwist narrative of creation in that God sets certain boundaries for human behaviour, as symbolised by the two trees in the centre of the Garden of Eden. These boundaries are not intended to inhibit the human being's freedom, but to protect it. Chaos and bondage erupt when humans transgress the boundaries set by God. Sin is the result of the human being's misuse of his freedom, and his opposition to God's grace. It leads to self-isolation and estrangement from God.

As noted earlier, sin does not totally destroy the image of God in the human, because it does not eradicate humanity's relationship with God. Despite the sinful nature of the human being God refers to man as His representative on earth, who was created after His image.[18] In Gen 9:6–7 the instructions of Gen 1:26–28 are repeated. The human still has the same responsibilities, as well as the freedom to respond to God. This does not mean that sin has no negative effects on human freedom. According to the Priestly narrative, God was forced to introduce authority.[19] The state is a divine institution that must reconcile freedom and law, and restrict freedom when it degenerates into licence. Freedom after all, is never an end in itself, but is always co-determined by the Will of God and the interests of fellow human beings, so that free responsibility and responsible freedom always go together.[20] The

15. Cf. Eph 4:24; 2 Cor 4:4; 3:18; Col 3:10.
16. Cf. 2 Cor 3:18.
17. Gen 1:28.
18. Gen 9:6–7.
19. Gen 9:5.
20. Van Wyk, "Etiek en menseregte," 36.

purpose of human authority is to uphold freedom. In Deut 17:20, for instance, the king is reminded that he is God's representative and therefore responsible to God. He is not allowed to exalt himself above ordinary Israelites. The accountability of leaders is also a recurring theme in prophetic literature.[21] The authority of the ruler is never absolute, nor indelible, but is regulated and validated by a criterion to which his subjects are also related, namely the law of God.[22]

In the Old Testament the exercise of political and social justice is consistently related to God's liberating work, which is the central indicative for social justice. This is particularly evident in the Pentateuch. Freedom is defined as a concrete reality that God creates through his acts of salvation—something the Israelites can enjoy as a gift from God. Justice is only possible if Israelites understand the nature of their new freedom.[23] The rights of the covenant people as well as the nature of the social order in Israel is founded upon God's liberation of Israel from the oppression of Egypt. God liberates Israel from slavery in Egypt and establishes a society which is the opposite of the system that Israel escaped from. One of the main characteristics of this new society is the freedom granted by God. Because He freed the Israelites from bondage, they may not oppress each other. In the deuteronomic Decalogue the Sabbath is a powerful symbol of Israel's exodus to freedom.[24] On the Sabbath Israelites must remember that God freed them from all forms of oppression and exploitation.[25] Even people who were not freed from the slavery in Egypt are granted freedom by the Sabbath Law by being granted free time in order to rest from their daily labor.[26]

The freedom God grants also extends to the weak in society, namely slaves, aliens, widows and orphans. The form of slavery in Israel differed significantly from the Graeco-Roman institution of slavery. In Deuteronomy slavery is seen as a form of welfare and never a permanent institution. The institution of slavery helped people socially and economically by bringing them into another family when they found

---

21. Isa 3:14; Hos 5:1; Micah 3.

22. Cf. Thielicke, *Theological Ethics: Politics*, 187.

23. Cf. Braulik, "Deuteronomy and Human Rights," 212.

24. Ibid., 213.

25. Deut 5:1–5.

26. Braulik, "Deuteronomy and Human Rights," 214.

themselves in distress.[27] Slaves belonged to the family and enjoyed the same juridical and religious rights as the rest of the family.[28] A slave oppressed and exploited could escape by flight without being prosecuted.[29] In the seventh year all Israelite slaves had to be freed. Resident aliens (*ger*) also belonged to a free class. Besides juridical rights, aliens also had the same religious rights as Israelites.[30] In Exod 23:9 and Lev 19:33, Israelites are commanded not to oppress aliens, because they themselves had been aliens in Egypt. Deuteronomy[31] gives this command a theological foundation: Israel has to imitate the love that God shows to all strangers.

Aliens, widows and orphans were particularly vulnerable to judicial arbitrariness and therefore special emphasis was placed on justice for them. This is a recurring theme not only in the Pentateuch, but also in the prophetic literature.[32] The demand for justice for the weak was often founded on the character of God, who protects the weak.[33] While the weak had to be protected, there were no laws that protected the privileged positions of the rich. The just treatment of the weak was God's main criterion for the righteousness of Israelite society.[34]

In the New Testament freedom primarily has a soteriological meaning. Christ frees the human from the bondage of sin, condemnation of the law and the righteous wrath of God through His expiatory work on the cross. In his relation to humankind, God becomes the liberating God. In their relation to God, those who are justified become free.[35] The human's existence becomes free, not by his denying his status as a child of God, but by his coming to a mature understanding of being a child that follows the example of Christ. By doing this he reflects the image of God and participates in the true humanity of Christ. This newfound freedom means that the human can now participate in the true destiny of humankind by serving God and fellow humans. Freedom is

27. Deut 15:12–15. Braulik, "Deuteronomy and Human Rights," 216.

28. Cf. Deut 15:6; Exod 21:26–27.

29. Deut 23:16.

30. Lev 17:8–13; 18:26.

31. Deut 10:18.

32. Cf. Deut 1:15; Amos 1:6–7.

33. Cf. Exod 23:7; Deut 15:9.

34. Exod 22:22–24.

35. Cf. Moltmann, *God for a Secular Society*, 198.

thus a positive concept. True freedom is *freedom for*, not only *freedom from*. An individual cannot pursue goodness in a way that is to the benefit of simply himself or herself, but he or she must also further the common good of the community.

The positive nature of freedom thus immediately suggests that Christian freedom has social implications. The social implications of Christ's work become particularly evident in the concept of the Kingdom, which expresses, amongst other things, the cosmological range of Christ's rule. In the coming of His Kingdom God reinstates His glory on earth, renews the human, and transforms His creation.[36] Christ's kingship extends not only to the church, but his redemptive work has implications for the entire cosmos.[37] His dominion should not therefore be understood in only a narrow soteriological sense, but also in a holistic cosmological sense, not only as a future eschatological reality, but also as a present, immanent reality that has political significance.

As a present reality the Kingdom relativises all earthly power in the light of Christ's kingship. Christ's death frees the individual from any ultimate claims on his life by society or the state.[38] Christians are called to be witnesses of the redemptive work of God in history by bringing deliverance for the poor and oppressed.

In the gospels the coming of Christ is closely related to deliverance for the poor. Christ came to bring them good news, to proclaim freedom for prisoners, recovery of sight for the blind, release for the oppressed, and to proclaim the year of the Lord's favour.[39] The gospel of the Kingdom that Jesus proclaimed is qualified as the *gospel of the poor* in various passages.[40] The beatitudes of both Mathew and Luke start by referring to the poor in spirit - they are the true heirs of the Kingdom of God. According to Ridderbos[41] the expression *poor of spirit* is derived from the theocratic, covenantal background of the Old Testament. The poor are the socially oppressed who experience injustice from those who enrich themselves. They long for God's liberation and place all

36. Braulik, "Deuteronomy and Human Rights," 31.

37. Cf. Col 1:16.

38. Cf. Pannenberg, *Human Nature*, 17.

39. Luke 4:18–19.

40. Luke 4:18, Matt 11:5, Luke 7:22.

41. Ridderbos, *De komst van het koninkrijk*, 170.

their hope for deliverance in God. They are the true bearers of God's promises, because they expect salvation from God and not from the world.[42] The gospels, in accordance with the Old Testament, qualify the poor in a social as well as a religious ethical sense.[43] The poor are those who are now hungry and mourning, because they are the victims of oppression.[44] Their longing for salvation entails a hunger and thirst for righteousness.[45] The righteousness for which they long is not of a forensic nature, but the righteousness which flows from the Kingdom of God and Christ's salvational reign.[46] Because they expect their deliverance from Christ, they are the true inheritors of the Kingdom of God. True subjection to Christ's reign means that the faithful must care for the physically handicapped and the hungry. Insofar as they care for the poor, they care for Christ Himself.[47]

Having reflected upon a theological understanding of freedom, we now proceed to discuss ways in which the Christian concept of freedom can function in an overlapping consensus.

Christian Freedom within an Overlapping Consensus

Liberalism's weakness is that it neglects the impact of sin on human life. According to Pannenberg,[48] liberalism rarely considers the degree to which the appeal to reason and to the common good is subservient to the self-interest of individuals and groups. Since liberalism does not take the need for liberation from sin seriously, the connection between religion and freedom has almost been obliterated, and the human has become the centre of his own life. In turn, the liberal idea of freedom has become shallow, because it has been abstracted from the actual social situation of those individuals who, because of their social conditions, are not in a position to claim for themselves the possibilities which theoretically should be open for everyone. Often people consid-

---

42. Ps 22:27, 37:11; Isa 11:4, 29:9.

43. Ridderbos, *De komst van het koninkrijk*, 171.

44. Cf. Matt 5:4–6.

45. Matt 5:6.

46. Ridderbos, *De komst van het koninkrijk*, 172.

47. Matt 25:34–36.

48. Pannenberg, *Human Nature*, 20.

ered free in a formal and legal sense do not experience true freedom because of their social situation.

Though the abovementioned biblical perspectives do not provide us with a blueprint for resolving conflict between freedom and equality, they do offer some conceptual clarity that may rectify the shortcomings in the liberal approach. According to a Christian perspective, freedom is part of the created structure of the human being, and is therefore an inviolable part of being human. True freedom does not find its expression in licence and anarchy, but in the privilege of participating in God's destiny for humankind. Freedom is, in the Christian view, a positive concept that is always exercised within the framework of justice. True liberty is not the freedom to do whatever one wants to do, but to do whatever one wants while respecting God and the basic rights of others.

The objection is often heard that a positive definition of freedom could lead to tyranny, because it imposes duties on people. However, positive freedom can't be rejected as unacceptable just because it may be distorted. Negative definitions of freedom can also become distorted. In fact, they often lead to individualism, anarchy and the deformation of social institutions. Positive freedom stresses that the rights of individuals and the community are related concepts and must be balanced in a way that does not violate the dignity of either the individual or the community. Individuals and community are related entities, and everybody has a responsibility regarding the existing laws, political justice, the need for a reasonable level of a welfare state, and so on. If the positive dimension of freedom is disregarded, a community will lack a sense of moral responsibility. Since Christian freedom is essentially a positive concept, it implies a close relationship between freedom and equality, because equality is the positive dimension of freedom. Western liberalism errs in overlooking the social dimension of freedom which can be found in the solidarity of people as a group.[49]

Because freedom is an inviolable characteristic of being human, basic liberties need to be taken for granted and are not subject to political bargaining or to the calculus of social interests. It is, however, not a requirement for a just society that all basic freedoms should be equally provided for. Rather, freedoms should be adjusted when they clash with each other, so as to provide one coherent scheme equally shared by all

49. Cf. Moltmann, *God for a Secular Society*, 123.

members of society.[50] Some freedoms are more essential than others, and more important for a coherent, stable society.

The following liberties can be considered as basic from a Christian perspective: Those that are closely linked to human dignity should enjoy preferential treatment, because they are related to the essential characteristics of the *imago Dei*. These include the right to be free from bodily control, torture, harm, serfdom, and exploitation. These freedoms form the core content of freedom. Without them there can be no freedom at all. The right to property is also a basic freedom, because it is essential for participation in the control of the means of production and natural resources. Since all people are created by God as his stewards to cultivate the earth, true freedom demands that humans have an inherent and equal right to own property. Where these rights of people are discarded, freedom is destroyed and oppression sets in. Liberty of conscience is a basic freedom essential to protect the human's relationship with God and his nature as a being free to act. Liberties such as freedom of thought and association are required to give effect to liberty of conscience. These rights thus go in tandem. Political liberties are important, because they are instrumental in preserving other liberties. They are also decisive for equality, because they protect the ability of people to negotiate for equal opportunities in society. It is therefore important that the political liberties of all citizens, regardless of their economic and social position, should be more or less equal so that everyone has a fair opportunity to hold public positions and influence the outcome of political decisions.[51]

Because the Christian concept of freedom is essentially positive in nature, it will also recognise substantive freedoms such as a right to housing, education, access to medical services, access to basic necessities such as food and water and social security. These rights can, however, not be seen as legally enforceable under all circumstances, because the realisation of such rights depends upon the availability of resources. Yet they can be acknowledged as Constitutional ideals. Judicial structures can expect the State to realise these rights according to the resources at its disposal.

---

50. Cf. Rawls, *Political Liberalism*, 295.

51. Ibid., 327.

A Theological Perspective on Equality

Equality is not part of the created structure of the human being, as is the case with freedom, because all people are not created with the same talents and abilities. All inequalities are therefore not necessarily unjust. The fallacy of extreme egalitarianism lies in its confusing equality with sameness, and trying to minimise individual differences by enforcing similarities upon people. Sameness and enforced homogeneity contradict the diversity of creation.

This does not mean that equality is not an important value in biblical theology. It is not an inherent quality of the human, but a status granted to people by God. People are created in the image of God and therefore are of equal worth. The relationship between male and female serves as a good example. The fact that the female was created with less physical strength than the male does not presuppose an unequal relationship between them, because all humans are in the image of God despite differentiated characteristics. This is illustrated in the Jahwist narrative in that the statement that the woman was taken from the man, is balanced in Gen 2:24 by the remark that the man will "cling" to the woman.[52] Male and female are further separately presented as being in the image of God.[53] In Gen 2:20–24 the woman is called the help, helper or equal of the man. This does not signify that the female is inferior to the male, but rather that she is a similar being with whom the male can commune.[54] The cultural mandate, furthermore, applies to male and female without distinction. This illustrates that God grants equal status and dignity to all people. Equality is, therefore, not a substantive concept that refers to sameness of ability and characteristics, but is the recognition of an equal status before God and each human being. It involves a complex interrelationship between persons.

According to the Jahwist narrative, unequal and oppressive relations are the result of sin. The male starts to rule over the female.[55] Not only gender relations, but all human relationships, are now characterised by oppression and exploitation.[56] The equality of all human beings,

52. Dreyer, "Vrou as beeld van God," 676–77.
53. Gen 1:27, 5:2.
54. Cf. Wentsel, *God en mens verzoend*, 630.
55. Gen 3:16.
56. Cf. Genesis 6.

who were created in the image of God, is denied because people do not honor their status before God and among one another.

Equality therefore requires justice. Though equality is not in itself justice it certainly resembles it, because equality implies the right not to be treated unjustly. The Old Testament refers to social and institutional justice in several passages, especially when the root words *sedeq* and *mishpāt* are used together. The prophets from the 8th century BC attributed the deterioration of social values and the oppression of the poor to the absence of *sedeq* and *mishpāt*.[57] Generally *sedeq* is a wider concept than *mishpāt*. It indicates the general principle of justice, while *mishpāt* is the concrete norm that is concretised in a juridical and institutional context.[58] Both concepts deal with obedience to a personal law because God prescribes it.[59] God himself is the norm, source and standard of all human justice.[60]

God is the embodiment of justice and His laws are just as well.[61] The human can only be righteous if he conforms to the norm stated by God.[62] God's jurisprudence is expressed by *shāpat*. It is both a characteristic and an act of God. He is the God of justice who is just.[63] In Jeremiah just behaviour is repeatedly related to true knowledge of Jahwe, while unjust behaviour occurs because man does not know the order of God. Restoration can only take place when human beings return to God.[64] It is clear that divine righteousness and human justice are not seen as two independent entities. Human justice is patterned after divine righteousness and can therefore not be comprehended without understanding God's action.[65]

The covenant is the framework within which the command to justice is concretised. In several passages in the Old Testament the covenant relationship between God and his people is described as a

57. Cf. Gosai, *Justice, Righteousness and the Social Critique of the Eight Century*, 244.

58. Eloff, *Staatsowerheid en Geregtigheid*, 121. Weinfeld, "Justice and Righteousness," 236.

59. Wessels, "Sosiale geregtigheid," 83.

60. Eloff, *Staatsowerheid en geregtigheid*, 113.

61. Cf. Ps 119:7; Deut. 4:6.

62. Gosai, *Justice, Righteousness and the Social Critique*, 51.

63. Eloff, *Staatsowerheid en geregtigheid*, 117.

64. Wessels, "Sosiale geregtigheid," 86–90.

65. Ellul, *Theological Foundation of Law*, 38.

relationship characterised by justice.[66] The various elements of the covenant, such as promises, responsibilities, and demands, are characteristics fundamental to the concept *ṣedeq*.[67]

The equality of the covenant community is founded upon freedom. The liberation from the oppression of Egypt forms the basis for the recognition that all Israelites are equal.[68] Never again should Israelites be enslaved. In His covenant God summons His people as a whole to a life of justice towards all, especially the poor, the weak and aliens.[69] The implementation of social justice is specifically the task of the king who acts as mediator between God and his covenant people. The king mediates between God's *ṣedeq* and *mishpāṭ* and man's *ṣedeq* and *mishpāṭ*.[70] Deuteronomic and prophetic literature in particular emphasize the importance of equality. Israel's recollection of its own bondage in Egypt prevented it from imposing radical inequality on racial groups or aliens. The basic structure of Israelite society had to be ordered in such a way that the interests of the weak were served. It is a recurring admonition in the Old Testament that the unfortunate, the widow, strangers and orphans must be justly treated, precisely because they have no other rights than what they have in the Lord.[71]

In the New Testament equality is understood within a soteriological context, as is the case with freedom. Christ is seen as the origin of equality.[72] Through His expiatory work He redeems sinners who do not deserve the grace of God and thus makes them children of God. Pauline theology in particular emphasizes that faith and salvation are gifts of God through Christ and cannot be attained by good works.[73] The human, therefore, cannot attribute his salvation to his own natural abilities. Because God redeems us through grace alone, believers may not exalt themselves at the expense of others, but must regard each other as equals and serve each other in humility as priests.[74] In Christ

66. Cf. Gen 18:19; Deut 6:25; Hos. 2:18.

67. Gosai, *Justice, Righteousness and the Social Critique*, 54, 69.

68. Ibid.

69. Cf. Ex 23:6, Ps 94:15, Prov. 12:5, Am 5:11.

70. Wessels, "Sosiale geregtigheid," 83.

71. Deut 24:17, Amos 4:1.

72. Gal 3:28; 1 Cor 12:13.

73. Cf. Eph 2:8–10; Rom 4:5.

74. Cf. Gal 6:2–4.

the boundaries between Jew and Greek, slave and freeman, male and female are transcended.[75] Paul even applies the principle of unity in Christ and equality before God to relations between parents and children, masters and slaves.[76]

In 1 Corinthians 12 and Ephesians 4 Paul supplements the principle of equality and unity in Christ with the doctrine of spiritual gifts. The *charismata* are God's spiritual gifts which He bestows upon believers through the Holy Spirit. These gifts must not be seen as private possessions, nor lead to self exaltation, but rather as collective assets which bind believers together in solidarity. The gifts in the congregation must develop in such a way that they benefit all, especially the weak and the poor.[77]

The early churches did not translate the practical result of the Pauline message on equality into a political programme of social equality. They consisted of a small entity with little political influence and the broader society was firmly based upon hierarchical convictions. We can also not directly transfer that which applies to the church to the secular realm.

This does not mean that the New Testament is irrelevant to discussions on social equality. Of particular importance is the close relationship between equality, justice and love in the New Testament. Several texts refer to the relation between Kingdom and justice. In Col 4:11 Paul addresses the believers as co-workers of God's Kingdom. In Rom 14:17 the Kingdom of God is called a Kingdom of justice, and in the Beatitudes the search for justice is related to citizenship of the Kingdom of God.[78] The search for the justice of God's Kingdom takes place within the cadre of love. Love entails that you treat others as you would like yourself to be treated.[79] Since God is love, love is the most important instrument in God's acts of justice. Without love there can be no justice, whereas true love will always be an instrument of justice.[80] True love does not only extend to close relatives, but is a general spirit of

---

75. Gal 3:28.

76. Eph 6:1–9.

77. 1 Cor 12:22, 23.

78. Matt 5:10.

79. Matt 22:39.

80. Du Toit, "'n Christelike beskouing van menseregte," 446.

humanity directed towards all people.[81] Love binds individuals into a community. Only where love and justice function in harmony, will true equality exist.

A Christian View of Equality in an Overlapping Consensus

Equality emanates from freedom and is intrinsically an expression of the social dimension of human freedom, because it always concerns just relations between two or more individuals. Without equality there will be no freedom for the weak and the marginalised. Moltmann[82] rightly states that rights to liberty cannot be protected in a world of gross political injustice and economic inequality. Freedom, similarly, is essential to any process in which equality is defined and secured.[83] We must, however, distinguish between natural inequality and normative equality. The fact that human beings are by nature unequal in ability does not lessen the importance of equality as a value, because the value of equality is normative in nature. Normative equality flows from the human's status of dignity bestowed upon him by God. Since all human beings are created in the image of God and share the same destiny, they are of equal worth and have the right to be treated fairly. Social policy needs to do justice to both natural inequality and normative equality. If actual inequalities are neglected, a totalitarian idealism is at work, distorting the concrete facts of life. If normative equality is disregarded, the humane criterion for social reform is disregarded.

In order to achieve this balance, we need to be clear on the reciprocal nature of freedom and equality and the basic demands of social justice. The premise of biblical literature is that justice demands that the interests of the weak be protected, because justice coincides with the exercise of love, compassion and solidarity. Thus the basic structure of society should be arranged in such a way that it maximises the primary goods available to the least advantaged.[84] At the same time natural inequalities should be kept in mind. Inequalities are acceptable, as long as they are not caused by injustice or social coercion, or are detrimental to the weak. The primary goods available to the weak can, as a matter

81. Cf. Eph 5:2; Rom 12:1; Phil 2:1–2.
82. Moltmann, *God for a Secular Society*, 120.
83. Cf. Dworkin, *Sovereign Virtue*, 122.
84. Cf. Rawls, *Political Liberalism*, 326.

of fact, only be maximised when natural inequalities are respected and people have the freedom to develop and employ their talents optimally. When natural talents are maximally utilised, natural inequalities can be used as collective assets that serve the well-being and cohesion of society as a whole. John Rawls's second principle of justice, called the difference principle, is particularly helpful here.[85]

Social and economic inequalities must satisfy two conditions. First, they must be attached to offices and positions open to all, under conditions of fair equality of opportunity, and second, they must be to the greatest benefit of the least advantaged members of society.

The implication of the difference principle is that the equal moral worth of persons does not entail that distributive shares need to be equal. Inequality is not immoral, as long as the progress of the most advantaged in society serves the well-being of the least advantaged. Even though certain actions might widen the gap between rich and poor, they would not be immoral if they still contribute to the enhancement of the least advantaged by maximising primary goods. However, actions that weaken the welfare of the least advantaged and reduce the primary goods available to them are always immoral, even though such actions might not be illegal.

Rawls' difference principle needs further elaboration. The interests of the weak cannot be addressed by supporting individuals only. Liberalism is naïve in suggesting that those inequalities perpetuated by association with groups can be overcome by freeing individuals from the group's disadvantages. Freedom and equality depend on state policy that empowers marginalised and diverse groups. Individuals cannot simply escape on their own from a stigmatised or weak group. Only group empowerment, not individual emancipation, advances social and economic equality.[86] To approximate greater equality the state will have to support and subsidise the weakest groups. Without state action some groups will remain weak.

85. Rawls, *Political Liberalism*, 291.

86. Cf. Beckley, "Empowering Groups and Respect for Individual Dignity," 17.

A Societal Framework for Resolving Conflict between Freedom and Equality

Though the abovementioned criteria provide some conceptual clarity, it would be naïve to think that conflict between equality and freedom can be solved by finding a single definition for both concepts which can guide us in pursuing the best kind of liberty and of equality simultaneously. A single definition will not help, because it will lack the content to give the necessary political guidance. Simply ascribing rights to different persons on the basis of their being created in the image of God will also not do, because politics needs to deal with the rights of many interrelated persons who are all created in the image of God. Instead, a more comprehensive philosophical framework is needed to deal with the challenges posed by the conflicting interests of freedom and equality.

The Autonomy of Societal Spheres

One of the essential features of the *Imago Dei* is that God created the human as a social and reciprocal being. In Gen 1:27 the *Imago Dei* is related to the human as being created as both male and female. The most basic social union is that between male and female in marriage. Around this relationship various social unions and societal spheres originate and develop. Genesis 1–11 describes the development of some of the basic social unions, such as marriage (2:24), family (4:1–2), commerce (4:20–22), the state (Gen 9:5-6), culture (4:21, 9:7) and technology (11:4).

Society consists of many different and divergent communities in which people lead different kinds of lives under different institutions.[87] Rawls is therefore correct when he describes society as a social union of social unions.[88] Yet social unions do not merely reflect human will and circumstance, but also God's structuring of creation. The various social unions display certain characteristics. To define the dynamics of social unions I shall utilise the insights of Neo-Calvinistic philosophy and the political philosophy of Michael Walzer.[89]

87. Cf. Nozick, *Anarchy, State and Utopia*, 312.

88. Rawls, *Political Liberalism*, 322.

89. Note that I am not interested in taking over the philosophical premises of Neo-Calvinism or Michael Walzer in all its dimensions. I am only focussing on those dimensions that I regard as helpful for understanding the dynamics of social unions.

The first characteristic of social unions is that they are governed by different creational laws. According to Neo-Calvinist philosophy God established a creational order of universal and constant law that governs the different societal spheres.[90] This means that within different societal spheres, certain immanent God-given norms control the processes involved. Though the human mind is perverted by sin, God's creational order remains in force and all humans are subject to these laws. God's creational laws are identifiable, even by people who do not believe in God, because God's laws are part of the structure of things. Non-Christians can inform and even correct our understanding of the creational order of things.

The creational laws governing social processes are not automatic, but demand human ethical decision-making. People are responsible agents who must implement God's norms in various spheres of human activity. It is therefore the task of human law to give actual form to God-given institutions.[91] They can either resist the nature and structure of things and deform or pervert their true meaning, or respect and positivise the God-given structure of things. In the various social spheres there are a variety of ways in which the God-given structure can be actualised. These are always human efforts to concretise moral norms and are consequently open to correction and revision.[92]

The second characteristic of social unions is that of sovereignty and universality. Neo-Calvinist philosophy distinguishes between sovereignty in its own sphere and universality in its own sphere. The principle of sovereignty in its own sphere states that each different institution and association has its own intrinsic nature, law of life and area of competence.[93] Internal laws and the law-making power of non-state associations are not delegated by the state. Law-making power is therefore plural in nature. Every sphere is autonomous in its own right and has its own sphere of power. The principle of sphere sovereignty corresponds with the Roman Catholic principle of subsidiarity, which means that authority should descend to the lowest level of society able to deal with a problem, and not be retained at a higher level. Dooyeweerd based

90. Haas, "Kuyper's Legacy for Christian Ethics," 342.

91. Cf. Ellul, *Theological Foundation of Law*, 107.

92. Haas, "Kuyper's Legacy for Christian Ethics," 343.

93. Dooyeweerd, *Roots of Western Culture*, 48.

the idea of sphere sovereignty on the notion that the various modal aspects of reality—the juridical, pistic, biotic aspects, and so forth—are irreducible. Each aspect is distinct in character and cannot be ignored or treated as if it were something else, without producing antinomies, contradictions or dialectical tensions.[94] This implies that no organisation qualified by one aspect can claim authority over others in their specific activity. Due to the intrinsic nature of differentiated spheres such as the family, the school, economic enterprise, science and art, they can, for instance, never be part of the state.[95] Whenever a principle valid in one sphere of life such as bios, or the economic factor, or the aesthetic law of form is absolutised and imposed upon other spheres, it becomes authoritarian.[96] In Marxism-Leninism for instance, the economic principle is no longer restricted to the economic sphere but determines the theme of all history.[97]

Whereas the principle of sovereignty in its own sphere guarantees the irreducibility of different spheres and protects their distinct laws, the principle of universality in its own sphere expresses the universal coherence of each aspect in its own particular structure.[98] According to Dooyeweerd every sphere has a nuclear moment that has an original meaning for that sphere alone. Yet there are other structural moments, or analogies, in each sphere that point to other sovereign spheres.[99] The nuclear moment in the institution of the church, for instance, is pistic in nature. A church is in essence a community of the faithful. Without faith the church will not be a church. Yet the church also exhibits other structural moments that do not define the essence of its existence, but are part of it, such as the juridical modality (maintaining internal order) and the aesthetic modality (singing of hymns). The juridical modality in the church is an analogy that relates the church to the state, because the nuclear moment in the state is the juridical modality. The state may have a say in church affairs as far as juridical affairs are concerned.

94. Dooyeweerd, *New Critique of Theoretical Thought*, 102–4. Cf. Marshall, "Dooyeweerd's Empirical Theory on Rights," 126.

95. Dooyeweerd, *Roots of Western Culture*, 56.

96. Cf. Thielicke, *Theological Ethics*, 120.

97. Ibid., 121.

98. Dooyeweerd, *Roots of Western Culture*, 46.

99. Cf. Dooyeweerd, *Encyclopedia of the Science of Law*, 103.

A third principle of society as a social union of social unions is that every sphere contains its own principles of distribution. Equality is a very difficult condition to realise and sustain over a period of time. Therefore it needs the application of complex rules of distribution in order to ensure that social goods don't become means of domination. In his book, *Spheres of Justice*, the political philosopher Michael Walzer looks at different types of norms which should govern the proper development of rights in different spheres of society. According to Walzer[100] proper distribution, i.e. processes of giving, allocating and exchanging, within pluralist society is only possible when it is recognised that every sphere of life has its own distributive principles. Goods have different meanings and different values in different societal spheres. All distributions are therefore just or unjust, relative to the social meanings of the goods at stake.[101] Domination occurs when social goods are monopolised and used in such a way that they are not limited by their intrinsic meanings.[102] However, when the distributive principles of every sphere of life are respected, a set of relationships is established that makes domination difficult.[103] A few examples will suffice: Communities distribute the social good of membership. The community selects members in accordance with its understanding of what membership means within their community and what sort of community they want to have. Admission and fair exclusion are the distributive principles at the core of the formation of communities. Without them there would be no communities of character—historically stable, ongoing associations of men and women with a special commitment to each other and some special sense of their common life.[104] As soon as the state disrespects the right of communities to self-determination and decides for itself which communities may be formed and what criteria must be followed, tyranny sets in.

The distributive principles of romantic relations are free choice and affection. Deserts or trade, for instance, cannot be distributive principles in romantic relations because love is not something that

---

100. Walzer, *Spheres of Justice*, 6.

101. Ibid., 8–9.

102. Ibid., 10–11.

103. Ibid., 19.

104. Ibid., 62.

can be deserved or bought. However, in the sphere of work, deserts is the distributive principle that determines appointments, because the labour market is determined by the supply of and demand for skills. If affection is seen as a distributive principle in the domain of labour, nepotism sets in.

The application of distributive principles in every sphere of life should be accompanied by procedural justice and just background institutions. The state has no right to decide whether communities may or may not be formed. Yet the state must see to it that the methods of exclusion used in the determination of membership are not unfair. When a person is prevented, for instance, from becoming a member of a group on the basis of his color, he is unfairly discriminated against. Deserts is the distributive principle at stake in the sphere of labour. Yet justice demands that all people must have a fair opportunity to apply for jobs. When distributive principles are not regulated by principles of justice, they might become open to abuse.

Practical Application in an Overlapping Consensus

Freedom can only be protected when the diverse natures and inherent principles of the different social unions are respected. The principle of sovereignty in own sphere is very important for maximising liberties, protecting autonomy and restricting the power of the state. Many particular communities have internal restrictions that encroach on freedoms which libertarians would condemn if they were enforced by the central state apparatus. Yet in a free society people may contract into various restrictions that the government may not legitimately impose on them.[105] A state which does not respect the autonomous nature of non-state institutions becomes totalitarian and oppressive. This does not mean that the state has no competence over other spheres of society. The juridical nature of the state demands that the state must regulate the external relations of societal entities and that it must act when other spheres of society act outside their fields of competence.

Respect for the various principles of distribution in different spheres is important for attaining equal distribution, because such principles automatically organise the major social institutions into one scheme of co-operation. They provide the framework within which

---

105. Cf. Nozick, *Anarchy, State and Utopia*, 320.

people might advance their ends. As long as the distributive principles of different spheres are respected, justice will enjoy priority over all other interests, because people accept their responsibilities as defined by the principles of each particular sphere and thus identify with interests broader than their own. A second aspect regarding these principles is important. Many distributional principles in the different spheres of life are liberties. Freedom of choice determines the distributive principle in romantic relations, freedom to self-determination determines the distributive principle for membership of communities, freedom of thought and speech are distributive principles in the political domain and ensure that all people are shown equal concern. In other words, freedom is a fundamental aspect of distributional equality and is in many cases the key to the protection of equality. Freedom and equality should therefore not be considered as conflicting values, but supplementing ones.

Conclusion

Freedom and equality are compatible values as long as they are used in a conceptually correct way, together with sensitivity to the principles that govern societal processes. They become conflicting values when their reciprocal natures are not respected, when they are not used to benefit people mutually, and when their meanings are defined without due consideration for social justice and the basic structures of society.

Dworkin rightly states that liberty and equality cannot conflict as two fundamental political virtues, because equality cannot even be defined except by assuming liberty to be in place, and cannot be improved by policies that compromise the value of liberty.[106] When we affirm our faith in liberty we also affirm the form in which we embrace equality.

---

106. Dworkin, *Sovereign virtue*, 182.

7

Theology and Otherness[1]

Introduction

WE CAN EXPECT THAT NEW RACIST THEOLOGIES WILL ARISE IN THE age of globalisation. The increasing migration of ethnic cultures to the Western world and the resultant feelings of xenophobia; the importation of foreign cultural artefacts from the West to Eastern, Asian and African countries at the expense of local cultures, folklore, traditions, customs, religions and language; cultural alienation; the erosion of collective social identity and the consolidation of new states creates an environment where racism may flourish.

Racism is the process whereby social groups categorize other groups as different or inferior on the basis of phenotypical characteristics, cultural markers or national origin.[2] A particular group's physical traits are seen as intrinsically related to its culture, personality and intelligence. These traits are perceived as innate and not subject to change.[3] People are consequently judged on the basis of their group membership and not on the basis of personal attributes. One of the main features of racism is that it often needs an ideology to provide its views with a non-negotiable and fixed status that will ensure the durability of ethnic inequality. As long as racist practises are not questioned a cohesive racial ideology is not necessary. However, when racist practises come

1. This chapter was originally published as "Christian Theology and Racist Ideology: A Case Study of Nazi Theology and Apartheid Theology," *Journal for the Study of Religions and Ideologies* 7.19 (2008) 144–61. Used by permission.

2. Castles, *Ethnicity and Globalisation*, 164. Cf. Van den Berghe, *Ethnic Phenomenon*, 29.

3. Marger, *Race and Ethnic Relations*, 27.

under attack, systematic racial ideologies are constructed in order to provide logical foundations for racial resentment that rationalize and legitimize patterns of dominance and subordination. Full-blown racist ideology, for instance, developed only after the emancipation of slaves when continued domination of blacks without the institution of slavery required further justification.[4]

Ideologies often use religion to provide their views with a fixed status. An ideology can be defined as a mode of thought that elevates a single aspect of life to an all embracing principle in terms of which the whole of reality is interpreted. This chapter specifically focuses on the role that pseudo-Christian theology played in the construction of the racial ideologies of Nazism in Germany and Apartheid in South Africa. It investigates the various functions that pseudo-theology performed in the construction of these ideologies, and it seeks to identify some common elements that are present in these ideologies and that might be used in future to justify racist ideologies.

It must be noted beforehand that this chapter focuses on distortions of Christian theology that were used to justify racism and does not attempt to blame the Christian religion as such for the construction of racist ideologies. Most Christian churches in Germany and South Africa fervently opposed Nazism and Apartheid.

The Use of Christian Theology in Racist Ideology

A distortion of religion can help ideologies to change the collective behaviour of people and reinforce an attitude of obedience and sacrifice. The racist ideologies of Nazism and Apartheid used religion to give it a divine commission and divine mission. These theologies were not authentically Christian. They contradict the essential principles of Christian universalism that rules out any kind of inequality on the basis of racial and ethnic difference. These theologies did not arise as responses to profound religious experiences or encounters with the numinous, but merely as ideas that, as a consequence of their social utility, have caught fire in the crucible of the modern consciousness.[5]

---

4. Cf. Marx, *Making Race and Nation*, 58.

5. Davies, *Infected Christianity*, 20.

When we compare the racist theologies that were used to justify Nazism and Apartheid it is evident that the methods, features and common elements are the same, though the ideological contents differ.

Creating Origin Myths

In order to justify an ethnically defined order, racial ideology needs to affirm or reinvent the past. A distorted vision of the past explains the present much more satisfactorily than do the real complexities of history. Both in Apartheid and Nazism theological constructions were used to create origin myths. These theological constructions were mixed with myths in a religious and scientific guise that explained the origins of peoples and the mystery of evil. The construction of origin myths were needed to create a sense of belonging and exclusiveness that would achieve the integration of a group. After all, the whole notion of *race* suggests a communality of descent or characteristics.

In Germany Neo-Romanticism endorsed the mystical Aryan race myth and in the process influenced German Protestantism. According to the earlier Romantics such as Fichte and Herder, language and life are bound together in an organic unity.[6] Language is an expression of the spiritual character, creative genius and soul of a nation. It is through language that an individual becomes conscious of himself, identifies himself with a people and develops his political and moral character.[7] True self-determination is only possible in the process of speaking a pure original language. Fichte distinguished between superior and inferior nations on the basis of language.[8] According to Fichte the German spirit is the bearer of all general values, because an intrinsic connection exists between the divine life of God and the mysterious inner life of the German nation.[9] German nationality is for Fichte something divine, an organ through which the eternal Spirit reveals itself.[10] Neo-Romanticism combined this view of the nation as an organic entity with the Aryan myth. The Aryans were supposedly an original white race whose place of origin was India and whose lan-

6. Cf. Fichte, *Fichtes Reden an die Deutschen Nation*, 72.

7. Herder, *Über den Ürsprung der Sprache*, 41.

8. Fichte, *Fichtes Reden an die Deutschen Nation*, 74, 75.

9. Ibid., 76. Cf. Davies, *Infected Christianity*, 30.

10. Cf. Fichte, *Fichtes Reden an die Deutschen Nation*, 76.

guage is at the basis of Latin, Greek, Persian and Sanskrit. The superiority of the Aryans becomes evident when their language is compared to the Hebrew-related Semitic languages. The original white race of Aryans migrated from India and founded empires wherever they came. They are the ancestors of the modern Europeans, in particular the Germans, who are the only people who speak the language of the *Urvolk* and who are in touch with their own spiritual and racial origins. Nazi ideologues such as Hitler and Rosenberg attributed the crises of post First World War Germany to the vitiation of the German people's racial heritage through intermarriage. Salvation entailed the recovery of that heritage through national programs of biological regeneration.[11] The Aryan myth established a somatic norm, not only in Germany, but all around Europe. Whiteness became the criteria of the value of human beings. German churches were soon infected by the Aryan ideology. In the period of 1933–1935 the German Christian faction supported the Aryan laws implemented by the state and called for Aryanization in the church as well as the state.

Whereas racist Europeans developed the Aryan origin myth, the Afrikaners of the nineteenth century regarded themselves as a people assembled, called and elected by God to serve Him in a continent of darkness and barbarianism. The doctrine of an elect people afforded the Afrikaners a means to create a new society. Theological ideology was integrated into the whole culture of the Afrikaner. The history of Israel was literally applied to Afrikaner history. The Afrikaners saw themselves as the covenantal people of God. As the Israelites were liberated from bondage to the Egyptians the Afrikaners were liberated by God from the bondage of the British. As the Israelites were led into the desert by God in search of the Promised Land, the Afrikaners were guided by God in the Great Trek to find their own promised land. As God made a covenant with Israel at Sinai, He made a covenant with the Afrikaners at Blood River.[12] The battles that the Afrikaners fought were not seen as black-white conflicts, but rather conflicts between believers and nonbelievers.[13] The election ideology that the Afrikaners developed was not authentically Christian. In both the Old and New Testament God's elec-

11. Cf. Hitler, *Mein Kampf*, 297.

12. These notions can clearly be seen in the speeches of Paul Kruger, an Afrikaner president of the ZAR. Cf. Du Plessis, *President Kruger aan die Woord*, 92–93.

13. Meiring, "Nationalism in the Dutch Reformed Churches," 58.

tion is portrayed as an action of God that transcends ethnic, cultural and gender divides.[14] Unfortunately, the Afrikaners' view of themselves as the elect nation of God's covenant was one of the root causes of segregation laws when the Union was formed in 1910.[15]

The abovementioned origin myths served one common goal: To strengthen nationalist and collectivist sentiments and consolidate group or national interests.

Idolising the In-Group

Origin myths sacralise the history of a group. The result is that the in-group is bestowed with a superior status. In Germany noted critical theologians, deeply influenced by the nationalistic and racialist influences of Romanticism and Idealism, attempted to reconcile Jesus with Germanism, and Germanism with Jesus.[16] Albert Schweitzer[17] states it as follows:

> Historical criticism had become, in the hands of most of those who practised it, a secret struggle to reconcile the Germanic religious spirit with the Spirit of Jesus of Nazareth.

Baur, for instance, combined Herder's idea that each group of people is animated by a single spiritual principle, with Hegel's idea that these spiritual principles are ordered into a narrative of progressive dialectical development.[18] According to Baur[19] history is the sphere in which the Spirit reveals itself concretely:

> Revelation is the act of the Spirit, in which an objective reality confronts subjective consciousness as an immediate given, and becomes for the subject the object of a faith whose content is the absolute idea.

Religion is essentially a relation of Spirit to Spirit, in which Spirit mediates itself with itself through the activity of thinking.[20] Baur dis-

---

14. Isaiah 56, Ephesians 2.

15. Cf. Baskwell, "Kuyper and Apartheid," 1274.

16. Cf. Davies, *Infected Christianity*, 35.

17. Schweitzer, *Quest of the Historical Jesus*, 310.

18. Cf. Snyman, "Racial Performance and Religious Complicity," 599.

19. Baur, "Lectures on the History of Christian Dogma," 298.

20. Ibid., 297–98.

tinguished three major historical epochs related to different groups of people that manifested different degrees of awareness of the Absolute Idea. The Oriental Jews lacked spiritual inwardness, but gave the world monotheism, although tinged with nationalism and particularism. The Western Greeks possessed spiritual freedom, but lacked an objective foundation in monotheism. From the Romans the Christians received universalism, allowing Christianity to unite the objective and subjective into an absolute religion. According to Baur Jesus purified the essential spirit of Judaism and Greece into the Christian religion which is the absolute religion and which is appropriate for the whole world.[21] Christianity, however, underwent its own spiritual development. Christian history is fuelled by the conflict between the Eastern servile legalism of Jewish Christianity (thesis) and the Western gospel of Pauline freedom (antithesis) that found its synthesis in Catholicism.[22] Embedded in Baur's theology is the racialist notion that Western Christian theology is the highest manifestation of the evolution of the Spirit, while Eastern Christian theology is permeated with servility, legalism and despotism. Baur, indeed, translated the racialist assumptions of Hegelian philosophy into Christian theology.

Racist theologians soon capitalised on Fichte, Hegel and Baur's idealistic thinking. Houston Steward Chamberlain (1855–1926) provided German nationalism with an elaborate racist theology. According to Chamberlain the Christian religion is the natural religion of the Aryan-Teutonic man. Judaism (thesis) gave rise to Jesus (antithesis), who negated Judaism to produce Christianity (synthesis). Jesus is the supreme symbol of the Aryan race and is the great opposite of the Semite. He will cure society of its Semitic sickness by overcoming materialism in the same way he has overcome the Pharisees.[23]

Paul Althaus and Emmanuel Hirsch combined the Fichtean concept of the *Volk* as a unity of similar-spirited men with the neo-Lutheran idea that the *Volk* is a product of divine ordinance. The result was that they absolutised the *Volk* to such a degree that the *Volk* became the medium of God's presence and therefore demanded unconditional obedience, discipleship and sacrifice.[24]

21. Snyman, "Racial Performance and Religious Complicity," 599–600.
22. Ibid., 600.
23. Chamberlain, *Foundations of the Nineteenth Century*, I:200, 211.
24. Cf. Davies, *Infected Christianity*, 47–48.

The German Christian Movement, who supported the Nazi Reich of Hitler, united in the 1930's around the figure of the Aryan Christ and the *Volk* as a divine ordinance. Jesus was pictured as an Aryan, the Old Testament and the writings of Mathew, Luke and Paul were discarded as Jewish, and the doctrines of sin and grace were rejected. Only a positive Christianity without the guilt of sin was fit for a great race.[25] Neo-Fichtean concepts of the German blood, race and soil were inserted into German theology. The heart of the people is the bond of blood that runs from generation to generation and determines the people's spiritual being. Inherited blood issues in race, so that reverence for race is a sacred obligation. The soil is the sanctuary in which God meets people and is therefore sacred.[26] Since God created blood, soil and race, and reveals Himself in blood and race, the German people have to cultivate a religion that flows from German soil, its own nature and from the German race.[27] The German Christians soon demanded that the visible organization of the church should correspond to the historical and *völkisch* divisions of the Christian world because it is only in their membership of the *Volk* that people can unite themselves with God. The German People's Church thus organised itself on the principle of one People, one Reich, one Faith.[28] As might be expected, the emphasis on blood also led to the notion that race must be kept pure and sound as if this were a commandment of God.[29] The result was that race was made the decisive criterion of church membership. Germany was seen as an elect nation, because of the special characteristics of the German people.[30]

J. D. du Toit was the first prominent Afrikaner theologian who provided a systematic biblical justification for the forced separation between groups. In a speech to a congress of an Afrikaner culture organisation called the *Federasie van Afrikaanse Kultuur*, he used the separation motive in the creation narrative of Genesis 1, the cultural mandate in Gen 1:28 and the story of the Tower of Babel as justifications for segregation. According to this view separation was one of

25. Cf. Bonkovsky, "German State and Protestant Elites," 132.
26. Cf. Frey, *Cross and Swastika*, 85–87.
27. Cf. ibid., 54, 70.
28. Cf. ibid., 119.
29. Cf. ibid., 120.
30. Cf. Davies, *Infected Christianity*, 30, 37.

God's creational motives from the start. In the same way that God separated lightness and darkness, He wills the separation between nations. His exegesis was strongly influenced by the idea that black is a symbol of degeneracy, baseness and evil, a sign of danger and repulsion, while whiteness is synonymous with being Christian. According to du Toit, God gave the command that humanity must fill the earth in Genesis 1:28 because he desired the earth to be filled with a great diversity of races and peoples. Instead humanity opted to disobey the creation principle of separation by staying together and building the Tower of Babel. God therefore decided to disperse humanity by force at Babel. From this du Toit concludes that a nation that God brings together may not be separated, while different nations may not be integrated with each other.[31]

Since the 1950s Apartheid theology used the philosophical perspectives of Neo-Calvinist Kuyperianism, neo-Fichteanism and the abovementioned creational motives to justify the privileged treatment of white people. The Dutch theologian Abraham Kuyper distinguished between various societal spheres each with their own internal laws and authority, which were not to be encroached upon by other spheres or authorities.[32] His intention with the principle of sphere sovereignty was to prevent power abuse by the state. South African neo-Calvinist philosophers, most notably H. G. Stoker, moved beyond Kuyper by applying the principle of sphere sovereignty, not only to societal spheres, but also to different cultural spheres that have their own structural principles and own unique destinies. According to Stoker[33] these cultural spheres find their origin and legitimacy in the creational ordinances of God with the result that the Afrikaner nation is sovereign in its own sphere and has an own calling and function that distinguishes it from other nations.

The Apartheid theology of the Dutch Reformed Church, especially its policies on mission, was also influenced by the neo-Fichtean view of the *Volk*. The history of the Afrikanervolk was seen as a form of divine revelation. Every nation is created by God with its own *soul* and

---

31. Du Toit, *Die godsdienstige grondslag oor ons rassebeleid.*
32. Kuyper, *Het Calvinisme*, 79.
33. Stoker, *Die stryd om die ordes.*

temperament.[34] However, the souls of all nations are not equally developed. The maturity of the soul of a nation depends on its exposure to the gospel. A hierarchical view of nations developed from this notion. Indigenous African nations that had little exposure to the gospel were nations of a lower order than Christian nations. Nations of a higher order may under no circumstances mingle with nations of a lower order, because this will vitiate their own values.[35]

These Kuyperian and neo-Fichtean perspectives were all combined in the 1974 Report of the Dutch Reformed Church: *Ras, volk en nasie en nasieverhoudinge in die lig van die Skrif*. The Report justified Apartheid on the principle of pluriformity. God's creation is characterised by plurality and differentiation and not homogeneity. The story of the Tower of Babel is a clear indication that the essence of sin lies in its seeking uniformity and integration. This is contrary to God's creative will that seeks unity in plurality.[36] The principle of pluriformity is then combined in the report with a Romanticist view of language that attaches a biological meaning to language. At Babel God created different languages so that every nation would develop its own culture. The differentiation in languages gave "character and momentum to the process of differentiation".[37] It necessarily leads to the division of humanity into different cultures, religions and races. Whenever a certain group is viewed as superior or is equated with goodness, theology and ideology enter the realm of dichotomic distinctions. The superiority of certain groups naturally presupposes the inferiority of other groups.

Identifying the Out-Group

Racism always implies that the superior group has the power to propose a definition of the *other* and to apply it to the subordinate group. Integral to racism is the consciousness of the tension between *we* as the *in*-group and *they* as the out-group.[38] Humans are subdivided into distinct hereditary groups that are innately different in their social

34. Cf. Nederduitse Gereformeerde Kerk, *Die NG Kerk in Suid-Afrika en rasseverhoudinge*, 8.

35. Cf. Kinghorn, "Die groei van 'n teologie," 94.

36. Cf. Nederduitse Gereformeerde Kerk, *Ras, volk en nasie*, 12–17.

37. Nederduitse Gereformeerde Kerk, *Ras, volk en nasie*, 15. (Own translation).

38. Cf. Vorster, *Ethical Perspectives on Human Rights*, 145.

behaviour and mental capacities and that can therefore be ranked as superior or inferior.[39] These dichotomic racial definitions help people to understand and cope with a complex world around them. The devaluation of others and the setting up of a particular group as a scapegoat raise self-esteem and provide explanations for life problems that are otherwise difficult to comprehend.[40] This creates an illusion of unity through the oppositional force of a symbolic *other* and it provides an instrument for defining belonging or exclusion that justifies the differential treatment of others.[41]

In Germany racial theology transformed the Jew into an evil principle that was seen as a threat to racial purity and Aryan survival. The Aryans and the Jews were transformed into antithetical symbols around which the conflicting elements in human existence were organised: for example: goodness and evil, life and death, beauty and ugliness.[42] Anti-Semitism became a cosmological religious principle. The German Christian Church condemned all associations with Jews, especially intermarriage, and even missionary work among Jews because this would allow the entry of foreign blood into the national body.[43] The German People's Church demanded during a demonstration in Berlin in 1933 that Christianity should emancipate itself from the Old Testament with its Jewish morality and that the Aryan paragraph, that allows only Aryans in the church, should be put into effect.[44] The Saxon's People's Church also rejected the notion of the Old Testament as primary revelation of God, since the specific morality and religion of the Jewish people had been transcended. The curse of God lies on the Jewish people because they crucified Christ.[45]

In nineteenth century colonial South Africa, the subjugation of indigenous peoples was often justified through the myth of the curse upon Ham's son Canaan (Genesis 9–10). Genesis 9–10 relates how Noah's sons reacted when they found him drunk. Shem and Japheth did

---

39. Marger, *Race and Ethnic Relations*, 27.

40. Staub, *Roots of Evil*, 17.

41. Cf. Crenshaw, "Race, Reform and Retrenchment," 550.

42. Cf. Davies, *Infected Christianity*, 61.

43. Little, "Church Struggle and the Holocaust," 26.

44. Cf. Frey, *Cross and Swastika*, 118.

45. Cf. ibid., 121, 122.

not look upon him, but covered their father, while Ham looked upon Noah and did not cover him. As a result Ham's son Canaan was cursed by Noah and told that he would be the servant of his brethren. Racist colonial theology viewed Ham as an African who transmitted his divine punishment to his descendants, who became servants to other people. This theological doctrine was a clear form of *eisegesis*, since there is no allusion in the Old Testament to the African characteristics of Ham.

Twentieth century Apartheid theology portrayed communism as the visible antithesis of Christianity. Communism was also viewed as the antithesis of Apartheid. The rejection of the social separation policies of Apartheid would necessarily imply the acceptance of an atheist communist worldview, because doctrines of social equality have their origins in communism.[46]

From the abovementioned it becomes clear that racist ideologies are obsessed with difference.[47] Their premise is the difference among and irreconcilability of different groups and their message is a message of love for the in-group and justified hatred of the out-group. By cultivating hatred against an out-group, the members of the in-group are encouraged to apply a perversely modified set of moral principles in their behaviour towards the out-group.

Creating Racial Rites and Symbols

Religious rituals, cults and symbols play an important role in giving racial ideologies a divine sanction and mystic image. They reinforce a sense of community and give racial ideology a transcendental character. These modified religious rituals and teachings often have little to do with traditional Christian teachings and morals. It is rather the appropriation of religious symbolism and exploitation of religious imagery that are important.[48]

The extreme German Christian movements deified the Führer in their Six Theses for German Christians, by describing him as a personal representative and revelation of Christ. Hitler was described as a true Messiah of the German People, a mediator between God and people, who required absolute obedience. National Socialism was described

46. Cf. Kinghorn, "Die groei van 'n teologie," 107.

47. Goldberg, "Racial Knowledge," 155.

48. Carmichael, *Ethnic Cleansing in the Balkans*, 90.

as the way of the Spirit that God wills for the Christian church of the German nation.[49] The blood flag symbolised the sacrificial blood necessary for the German Reich's victory. It was an obvious allegory of the cross.[50]

In Apartheid theology and Afrikaner nationalism the Day of the Covenant had a very important symbolic meaning. The Day of the Covenant originated in a vow which the *Voortrekkers* took several days before they engaged in an armed conflict with the Zulus on December 16th, 1838. The *Voortrekkers* vowed that if God granted them victory, they would annually commemorate this day as a Sunday. The vow was initially not celebrated by the whole Afrikaner community, possibly because it was understood as a promise binding the individual *Voortrekkers* who had partaken in the battle and their families and descendants, without committing the whole Afrikaner community that was scattered around the southern parts of South Africa.[51] However, the status accorded to December 16th among Afrikaner people rose considerably with growing British pressure on the Afrikaner republics at the end of the nineteenth century and the rise of Afrikaner nationalism in the early twentieth century. The day was used by Afrikaner nationalists, such as Paul Kruger, to compare the situation of the Afrikaner with the situation of Israel in the Old Testament.[52] The events at Blood River were seen as a sign that the Afrikaner nation was the elect nation of God. In the Apartheid era from 1948 onwards the symbol of the Day of the Covenant was used to emphasize the belief in the special calling of the whites in South Africa on behalf of Christendom, and of the necessity to protect the privileged position of whites.[53]

Creating Utopian Final Solutions

Most racial ideologies share the modernist conviction that human conditions can be improved by reorganising human affairs on a rational basis. They come into their own in the context of a design of the perfect society and the intention to implement the design through planned and

49. Cf. Frey, *Cross and Swastika*, 129.

50. Taylor, *Prelude to Genocide*, 179.

51. Kistner, "The 16th of December in the Context of Nationalist Thinking," 74.

52. Ibid., 74, 79, 80.

53. Cf. ibid., 86.

consistent effort.[54] The rationale behind racist ideology is that certain categories of human beings cannot be incorporated in the social order because they cannot be reformed. In fact, if these categories of people are excluded from society human progress will be possible.

Religion is often helpful in creating utopian solutions that offer hope for a new world order, and restore the pride of a group. In the pseudo-theology of the German Christians the utopian design was the thousand year Reich—the kingdom of the liberated German Spirit. The German Reich was seen as the start of a new utopian eschatological dispensation.[55] It was a kingdom that had no room for anything but the German Spirit.[56] The Nazi designers of the perfect society split human life into worthy and unworthy, the first to be lovingly cultivated and given *Lebensraum*, the other to be excluded.[57] Apartheid theology sought a geographical reconstruction of society where each group was to develop within its own confines. Different races after all have different potentials. Technological civilisation was the expression of the white race alone, while black peoples expressed themselves through tribal cultures. Through the establishment of homelands for all the black tribes a utopia would be created whereby different nations would develop in peace alongside each other. Apartheid would be the expression of God's original plan for His creation, that is, a society that recognises pluriformity and diversity by separating different cultures and races.

The utopian social order is always defined in contrast to an existing order that must be destroyed. This makes racial ideologies very dangerous. Violence is often seen as a legitimate way to change the social order. In extreme cases such final utopian solutions might even lead to genocide.

Evaluating Common Elements in Nazi and Apartheid Theology

Though Apartheid theology and Nazi theology differed in the doctrines they proclaimed, and used various hermeneutical interpretative methods of Scripture that range from critical to fundamentalist methods,

54. Baumann, "Modernity, Racism, Extermination," 216.

55. Vorster, "Preventing Genocide," 387.

56. Cf. Baumann, "Modernity, Racism, Extermination," 216.

57. Ibid., 217.

they did contain certain common theological presuppositions. It is important for Christianity to clearly identify these common features in corrupt pseudo-Christian theology and to address the factors that gave rise to it. Christian theology especially needs to ask itself: In what way did hermeneutical methods of interpretation used within Christian theology provide opportunities for racists to distort the Christian religion?

Collectivist Anthropology

Racist theology thinks in collectivist terms, and not in individual terms. At the heart of racist theology lies the definition of the human being as a racial being who derives his identity from a particular racial group. Race becomes the norm according to which social relations are structured. A peaceful co-existence between different groups of people within the same environment is viewed as impossible, because different races and people are basically irreconcilable. In Nazi-theology pure Aryan descent became the criterion for establishing the value of a human being and created a sense of exclusiveness that integrated and strengthened the group. Aryan descent and the German Volk actually became something divine, an organ through which God revealed Himself. The individual's life was seen as only having meaning through his belonging to the group. The Afrikaners' notion of themselves as the elect people of God, in a similar way attached the worth of the individual to the group he belonged to. Mixed descent and racial intermarriage was seen as an abomination in both Nazi and Apartheid theology.

Due to its collectivist premises racist theology thinks in terms of stereotypes and generalisations, and not in terms of the needs of individuals. Whenever the individual comes into view, it is as a member of a race, group or nation. The interests of the group are always more important than the interests of the self. This is a distortion of the Bible, which is the most authoritative source in Christianity. The Bible proclaims the unity of mankind that finds its origin in its creation by God.[58] Every individual possesses an inherent dignity, because all human beings were created in the image of God. Any notion of the superiority or inferiority of people due to gender, class, race, culture, ethnicity or

---

58. Cf. Gen 1:28, 5:1–2, Acts 17:26.

religion distorts the biblical view of the human.[59] Vorster[60] rightly states that the scope of the salvation in Christ depicts in Scripture the unity and equality of humankind. The reconciliatory work of Christ has no social preconditions, because Christ preached reconciliation irrespective of social divisions. This is explicitly stated in passages such as Gal 3:28, Isaiah 56, Matthew 28 and Ephesians 2.

The Identification of the Church with an Ethnic Group

Racist theology characteristically identifies the true church with a race or ethnic group. Apartheid theology, for instance, held that the church should not transcend the cultural and racial boundaries that God set between nations. In the same way that God revealed Himself through Israel, He reveals Himself to a particular nation through the church of that nation. The only difference between the Old and New Testament is that God now uses various churches within various nations.[61] In the theology of the German Christians the church was equated with the *Volk*, because the *Volk* is the organ through which the Spirit of God reveals itself.

However, this is again a distorted form of Christianity. In Scripture the church is not seen as the expression of the nation, it is the Body of Christ. Faith, not national descent, is the prerequisite for being a member of the Body of Christ. De Gruchy[62] rightly asks:

> The focus of redemption in the Scripture is the people of God. Can we then make use of the Christian gospel as a tool in the liberation of an ethnic group?

Vorster rightly states that the New Testament is the story of the divine ingathering of nations into a single community.[63] The universal morality that Christ preached extended to the concept of the church as a catholic community. According to the gospel of Matthew, Christ gave His disciples the command to preach the gospel to people of all cultures, nations

---

59. Vorster, *Ethical Perspectives on Human Rights*, 152.

60. Ibid., 153.

61. Nederduitse Gereformeerde Kerk, *Die NG Kerk in Suid-Afrika en rasseverhoudinge*, 37.

62. De Gruchy, *Church Struggle in South Africa*, 166.

63. Vorster, *Ethical Perspectives on Human Rights*, 153.

and groups and to make them members of the church.[64] The Church of Christ therefore does not negate nationality, masculinity or femininity, but transcends these in Christ.[65] The basic unity of the faithful in Christ becomes visible in the church as a multi-cultural, multi-national and multi-racial community. The catholic nature of the church lays the duty on the church to cultivate catholic personalities that embrace otherness. Ethnicism, racism and prejudice are fundamentally opposed to the basic message of the Christian Gospel.[66]

History as a Form of Divine Revelation

The absence of legality in racist ideology necessitates an appeal to a higher legality that is founded upon history. A common feature in racist theologies is that the history of a group is regarded as a form of divine revelation. Racial theology in Germany, for example, had its roots in a natural theology that developed over a period of two hundred years in German Protestantism. It was strongly influenced by the panentheïstic views of Hegel who saw history as part of the being of God. Critical theologians such as Baur and Strauss utilised Hegel's views. The German Christians held that, in addition to Jesus Christ, God revealed himself in the history of the National Socialist Revolution, in German blood, race and soil and in the messianic personality of Adolf Hitler.

Nineteenth century and early twentieth century Afrikaner theology believed that God revealed Himself in the history of the Afrikaner nation in the same way that he had revealed Himself in the history of Israel. The Afrikaner nation therefore had a divine calling. Prime Minister D. F. Malan[67] stated it as follows:

> The history of the Afrikaner reveals a determination and definiteness of purpose which make one feel that Afrikanerdom is not the work of man but of God.

Late twentieth-century Apartheid theology was characterised by a progressive notion of history. History is the process of the unfolding of God's original creative will. Because we can see the providence of God

---

64. Matt 28:16–20.

65. Cf. Gal 3:28.

66. Vorster, "Preventing Genocide," 391.

67. Kistner, "The 16th of December in the Context of Nationalist Thinking," 85.

in history, history is the revelation of the will of God. The separation of nations, and therefore the policy of separate development, is part of the unfolding of God's original creational plan of pluriformity in creation.

As soon as history is regarded as a form of revelation, faith and culture are harmonised and symbols of religion and forms of civilisation are identified with each other.[68] This opens the door for a subjective kind of theology that can easily degenerate into an ethnic theology. By "subjective theology" is meant a theology that is not faithful to the official scriptures and doctrines of a religion, but is based upon subjective perceptions, feelings, intuitions and interpretations of events and history. It leads to views, conclusions and interpretations that cannot be measured against an objective standard.

The Assimilation of Myths

Racist theology is eclectic in nature and is characterised by the appropriation of myths. The most common myth in racist theology is the notion of blood purity. For the nation to fulfil its divine destiny its must be isolated from admixtures that would dilute its purity. Nazi theology appropriated the Aryan myth, while Apartheid theology cited, without due regard for context, Old Testament texts that prohibited intermarriage between the Israelites and other nations to support the mythical notion of blood purity. Humans, however, operate within a genetically open system. Because human genes are interchangeable there exists an unbounded variety of physical types among the peoples of the world.[69]

The question is: Why does racist theology depend so much on myths? Racist theology is permeated with myth, precisely because the doctrine of racialism is a myth itself. Myths persist because they make the present more comprehensible by locating its origin in the past, thereby providing simple explanations to complex problems. They explain the unexplained, and fill the gaps in racist discourse, that authentic science and theology do not do. It is specifically the assimilation of myth and theology that makes racist theologies pseudo-theology and not authentic theology. Racist myths differ, amongst other things, from authentic theology in that they strengthen a particular racial ideology by polarising people, demonising opponents and justifying the

68. Cf. Davies, *Infected Christianity*, 117.

69. Cf. Marger, *Race and Ethnic Relations*, 19–20.

in-group. This stands in stark contrast to an authentic biblical Christian theology that is reconciliatory in style.

Conclusion

Because of the rise of racist and xenophobic behaviour worldwide, it is important for Christianity to clearly identify the common character-istics of racist theology and to educate its adherents on the difference between authentic theology and pseudo-theology, so that they will not fall prey to destructive forms of religion that encourage racism. In Nazi theology and Apartheid theology a distorted form of Christian religion was used to create origin myths, idealise the in-group, identify the out-group, to create racial rites and symbols and to produce utopian final solutions. It also shared some common theological presuppositions such as a collectivist anthropology, the identification of the church with an ethnic group, the divination of a specific group's history and the as-similation of origin myths. Apartheid theology and Nazi theology are, indeed, important case studies and help us to learn from mistakes made in the past.

8

Economics and Freedom[1]

Introduction

MILTON FRIEDMAN WAS ONE OF THE MOST INFLUENTIAL POLITI-cal economists of the twentieth century. He received the American Economic Association's John Bates Clark Medal in 1951, the Nobel Prize for Economics in 1976, and the United States' Presidential Medal of Freedom and the National Medal for Science in 1988. Friedman made a great impact on the discipline of economics as a monetary theorist, applied econometrician and narrative economic historian. He is widely credited for his contribution to modern labour economics and for changing the direction of macroeconomic theory.[2] Friedman's influence was not restricted to the academic discipline of economics, but also extended to the realm of politics. He acted as an adviser to Barry Goldwater, Augustine Pinochet, Richard Nixon, and Ronald Reagan, and became politically the most influential economic theorist of the last quarter of the twentieth century. The economic programmes of Ronald Reagan and Margaret Thatcher incorporated four neo-liberal elements that Friedman strongly campaigned for: 1) lower rates of taxation; 2) lower state contributions; 3) a free market instead of state regulation of industry and 4) the stable growth of the amount of money in circulation.[3]

1. This chapter was originally published as "A Deontological Critique of Milton Friedman's Doctrine on Economics and Freedom," *Journal for the Study of Religions and Ideologies* 9.26 (2010) 163–88. Used by permission.

2. Laidler, "Milton Friedman—A Brief Obituary," 373.

3. Küng, *Global Ethic*, 190.

This chapter is concerned with Friedman's core beliefs on politics, economics and freedom that are mainly found in his books *Capitalism and Freedom* (1962), *Free to Choose* (1980, co-authored with his wife), and *Tyranny of the Status Quo* (1984). An ethical re-appraisal of Friedman's views on politics, economics and freedom is particularly important at this time. Many analysts attribute the 2008 financial crisis directly to the neo-liberal deregulatory economic policies that were adopted since the 1980's by Western countries such as Britain and the United States. It's argued that these deregulatory measures led to irresponsible lending by banks, unethical practices in stock markets, and a culture of spending among consumers that in turn caused a global credit crunch.

Aim and Method

The first section of this chapter will discuss Milton Friedman's views on economics, politics and freedom. The historical origin of his thinking will be discussed as well as his perspectives on the relation between capitalism and freedom, the role of self-interest in the economy and the neutral nature of markets, his understanding of equality and the social responsibility of business. The second section will provide an immanent ethical critique on Friedman's thinking. Immanent criticism is a form of critique that endeavours to penetrate the premises of a thinking system and to reveal anomalies in that system. The last section will attempt to define from a Christian ethical perspective some key principles that are needed to reform the free market economic system. It will be argued that economics and social responsibility cannot be separated, that moral parameters need to be applied to the free market economy, and that the ecological impact of economic actions need to be taken seriously.

Friedman's Doctrine on Economics and Freedom

Friedman's views on politics, economics and freedom can be characterised as neo-liberal. Neo-liberalism emerged in the 1940s in reaction to the British Keynesian state, the New Deal welfarism in the United State and socialism in Europe. Intellectuals such as F. A. Hayek, Ludwig von Mises, Alexander Rüstow, and Michael Polanyi argued that in order to oppose these collectivist trends liberalism had to undergo a major process of intellectual reinvention where classic liberal tenets were re-interpreted on a new ideological terrain.[4] The Mont Pelerin Society was established in 1947 as the international meeting ground for academics and intellectuals who were broadly liberal in their views, and who were critical of collectivism. Their aim was to reinvent a coherent liberal philosophy for the twentieth century. Milton Friedman attended the founding meeting as a representative of the United States. It was here, under the influence of the philosophical radicals—Dicey, von Mises, Hayek and Simons—where Friedman's views on politics and economics took shape. He spent the rest of his career opposing the interventionist strategies and powers that achieved their optimum configuration in the period during 1945–1973. During this period, Keynesianism, was regarded as the most effective economic and political strategy for capitalism. The state assumed a variety of responsibilities and deployed fiscal and monetary policies to stabilize business cycles and demand conditions.[5] Friedman articulated his scepticism of organised capitalism most vividly in his 1962-book *Capitalism and Freedom* where he criticised twentieth century liberals for betraying freedom by regarding welfare and equality as either prerequisites of or alternatives to freedom.[6]

By the end of the 1980s neo-liberalism had, largely due to the efforts of Friedman, successfully redrawn the terms of the debate, sidelining both Keynesianism and socialist alternatives. It became the dominant paradigm that shaped the economic policies, not only of the United States, but also of international agencies.

Capitalism and Freedom

In his book *Capitalism and Freedom* Friedman argues that economic freedom is an end in itself and also an indispensable means toward the achievement of political freedom.[7] Capitalism founded on voluntary exchange among well informed agents is, according to Friedman, the only economic system that can guarantee true political freedom. By enabling people to cooperate with one another without coercion or

4. Turner, "Rebirth of Liberalism," 67.

5. See Smart, *Economy, Culture and Society*, 81.

6. Friedman, *Capitalism and Freedom*, 6.

7. Ibid., 8.

central direction, it reduces the area over which political power is exercised.[8] Capitalism provides a firm foundation for the maintenance of freedom where it already exists and a powerful impetus for its development where it does not exist, because bilateral voluntary exchange creates gains for both parties, and the more widespread its use, the more widespread are its gains.[9] Market economies in which consumers are free to choose are, therefore, both more efficient and ethically superior to command and control economies.

Friedman strongly believed that the scope of government must be limited. While government promises to preserve freedom, and may act as an instrument to that end in certain respects, it simultaneously represents a concentration of power that constitutes a threat to freedom. The government is unable to respond to, nurture or enhance the variety and diversities of individual action. Governmental power thus needs to be dispersed and decentralised so that freedom can be preserved.[10] A market economy is able to limit governmental power, because economic power can be dispersed.[11] By relying primarily on voluntary co-operation and private enterprise the private sector becomes a check on the powers of the governmental sector.[12] Friedman deplored state intervention in free market economies because these so-called protective measures are only a means to exploit the consumer.[13] Tariffs, restrictions on international trade, high tax burdens, regulatory commissions, government price and wage fixing, and a host of other state interventions only give individuals an incentive to misuse and misdirect resources. To Friedman the Great Depression was, far from a sign of the inherent instability of the private enterprise system, a testament to how much harm can be done by mistakes made by a few men when they wield vast power over the monetary system of a country.[14] Government must not be assigned any functions that can be performed through the market because voluntary co-operation is then substituted with coercion.[15] The

8. Friedman and Friedman, *Free to Choose*, 21.

9. Laidler, "Milton Friedman—A Brief Obituary," 375

10. Friedman and Friedman, *Tyranny of the Status Quo*, 42, 199.

11. See Butler, *Milton Friedman*, 207.

12. Friedman, *Capitalism and Freedom*, 3.

13. Friedman, *Free to Choose*, 62.

14. Ibid., 50.

15. Ibid., 38, 39.

role of government is to do something that the market cannot do for itself, namely to determine, arbitrate and enforce the rules of the game. Its major function is to preserve law and order, to prevent coercion of one individual through another, to enforce private contracts, to define the meaning of property rights and to enforce it, to foster competitive markets and to provide a monetary framework.[16]

Friedman proposes that the public sector must become more free-market orientated by being exposed to competition and the conditions of demands and supply. The injection of competition into the educational sector would for instance promote a healthy variety of schools and also introduce flexibility into the schooling system. Centralization in schooling has meant larger size units, a reduction in the ability of consumers to choose and an increase in the power of producers.[17] The benefits of a free market approach would be to give parents greater control over their children's schooling and to make the salaries of school teachers responsive to market forces. The size of a school would be determined by the number of customers it attracts, not by politically defined geographical areas.[18] This is also true with regard to the medical sector. Private enterprise can conduct medical affairs more economically than can government.[19]

The Role of Self Interest in the Economy and the Neutral Nature of Markets

In his attempt to help re-invent liberal philosophy Friedman adopted the philosophical notion of Adam Smith that individuals in a free market economy are led by an invisible hand to promote an end which was no part of their intention. The basic hypothesis of the invisible hand argument is that a social outcome which is elusive when pursued directly can sometimes be brought about by arranging for the individual members of a society to pursue an assortment of more immediate and more manageable objectives, perhaps even objectives which give every appearance of being at odds with that outcome.[20] According to

16. Ibid., 2, 27. See Butler, *Milton Friedman*, 204–6.

17. Friedman, *Free to Choose* 191.

18. Ibid., 199.

19. Ibid., 144.

20. Macleod, "Invisible hand Arguments," 103.

Friedman unintended mutual benefit emerges in a free market from the complex interactions of individuals in pursuit of their self interest, because, so long as cooperation is strictly voluntary, no exchange will take place unless both parties do benefit. By pursuing his own interest the individual promotes the well being of society more effectually than when he really intends to promote it through altruistic measures.[21] The central defect of welfarism, according to Friedman, is that it seeks through government to force people to act against their own immediate interests in order to promote a supposedly general interest.[22] At the heart of the welfare state lies the use of force because it takes away from some to give to others, making people who could have become self-reliant individuals, wards of the state. Civil liberty is thus seriously threatened.[23]

The promotion of self interest, in contrast, is one of the strongest and most creative forces known to man and is linked to people's longing to live according to their own values.[24] With the notion of self interest Friedman does not mean myopic selfishness. It is whatever a participant has an interest in, whatever he values and whatever goals he pursue.[25] The great virtue of a free society is that it permits these interests full scope and does not subordinate them to the narrow materialistic interests that dominate the bulk of mankind. That is why capitalist societies are less materialistic than collectivist societies.[26]

According to Friedman[27] the central feature of the market organisation of economic activity is its neutrality. The outcome of the market is an unintended consequence of the complex articulation of a multiplicity of individual decisions, unanticipated conditions and unforeseeable circumstances.[28] A competitive market is in essence impersonal. No one participant can determine the terms on which other participants shall have access to goods and jobs. The price mechanism is the mechanism that performs this task without central direction, without

21. Ibid., 133. Friedman, *Free to Choose*, 31.
22. Friedman, *Capitalism and Freedom*, 200.
23. Friedman, *Free to Choose*, 149.
24. Ibid.
25. Ibid., 47.
26. Ibid., 201.
27. Ibid., 14–15, 119.
28. See Smart, *Economy, Culture and Society*, 83.

requiring people to speak to one another or to like one another.[29] Prizes perform three functions in organising economic activity: first they transmit information, second they provide an incentive to adopt those methods of production that are least costly and thereby use available resources for the most highly valued purposes, third they determine who get how much of the product.

The market also prevents one person from interfering with another. The consumer is protected from coercion by the seller because of the presence of other sellers with whom he can deal, while the seller is protected from coercion by the consumer because of other consumers to whom he can sell. The employee is protected from coercion by the employer because of other employers for whom he can work. The market does this impersonally and without centralized authority. An impersonal market separates economic activities from political views and protects men from being discriminated against in their economic activities for reasons that are irrelevant to their productivity. No one who buys bread knows whether the wheat from which it is made was grown by a Communist or Republican.[30]

Capitalism and Equality

Friedman does not view equality as an alternative to or prerequisite for freedom. It is rather a corollary side effect of freedom. The heart of the liberal philosophy is a belief in the dignity of the individual, in his freedom to make the most of his capacities and opportunities, subject only to the provision that he does not interfere with the freedom of other individuals to do the same. This implies a belief in the equality of men in one sense, and in their inequality in another.[31] Each man's equal right to freedom is an important and fundamental right precisely because men are different and one man will want to do different things with his freedom than another. The liberal will therefore distinguish sharply between equality of rights and equality of opportunity, on the one hand, and material equality or equality of outcome on the other. Material equality is a desirable by product of a free society but not its major justification.

29. Friedman, *Free to Choose*, 33.
30. Ibid., 21.
31. Ibid., 195.

Seen from this perspective, capitalism actually promotes equality because it is based on the principle of voluntary exchange, it provides opportunities, allows for social mobility and it distributes the benefits of free enterprise widely. No economic system in history has improved the welfare of human beings more than capitalism. It has led to less inequality than alternative systems of organisation and has greatly lessened the extent of inequality. Though the capitalist principle of payment in accordance with product can be, and in practise is, charac-terised by considerable inequality of income and wealth, it is, according to Friedman, frequently misinterpreted to mean that capitalism and free enterprise produce wider inequality than alternative systems and, as a corollary, that the extension and development of capitalism has meant increased inequality.[32] The great achievement of capitalism has not been the accumulation of property, it has been the opportunities it has offered to men and women to extend, develop and improve their capacities.[33] Equality should not be measured by differences in levels of living between the privileged and other classes, but by the steady improvement in the level of the well-being of the poor, even if their relative economic position continues to decline.[34] Literal equality of op-portunity is not possible and it should not be proposed as a literal ideal. Equality of opportunity simply spells out in more detail the meaning of personal equality and equality before the law. Like personal equality, it has meaning and importance precisely because people are different in their genetic and cultural characteristics, and hence want to pursue different careers. In contrast to equality of outcome that reduces liberty for all because it wants to achieve fair shares for all, equality of oppor-tunity is an essential component of liberty because it enhances liberty.[35]

According to Friedman capitalism has reduced social discrimina-tion significantly through market orientated principles. The preserves of discrimination in any society are the areas that are most monopo-listic in character, whereas discrimination against groups of a particu-lar color or religion is least in those areas where there is the greatest freedom of competition.[36] There is also an economic incentive in a free

32. Ibid., 168.
33. Ibid., 169.
34. See ibid., 171.
35. Ibid., 163–64, 166.
36. Ibid., 109.

market to separate economic efficiency from other characteristics of an individual. A businessman or an entrepreneur who expresses preferences in his business activities that are not related to productive efficiency is at a disadvantage compared to other individuals who do not have such preferences.[37]

Friedman's conclusion on equality is that a society that puts equality ahead of freedom will end up with neither equality nor freedom. The use of force to achieve equality will destroy freedom, and the force introduced for good purposes will end up in the hands of people who use it to promote their own interests. A society that puts freedom first will end up with greater freedom and greater equality, because equality is a by-product of freedom.[38] Freedom means diversity but also mobility. It preserves the opportunity for today's disadvantaged to become tomorrow's privileged, and in the process enables almost everyone to enjoy a fuller and richer life.[39]

The Social Responsibility of Business

Friedman wrote a very influential essay published in the *New York Times* on 13 September 1970 with the title, "The social responsibility of Business is to increase its profits." This article expanded on a chapter in his 1962 book "Capitalism and Freedom" and is consistent with his philosophical view that an economy ought to be driven by self interest. The essay's premise is that business only has one responsibility—to use its resources and engage in activities designed to increase its profits so long as it stays within the rules of the game, which is to say, engages in open and free competition, without deception or fraud. Few trends would, according to Friedman, so thoroughly undermine the very foundation of a free society as the acceptance by corporate individuals of a social responsibility other than to make as much money for their stockholders as possible.[40] A corporation is an instrument of the stockholders who own it. Executives of a public corporation have a fiduciary responsibility to the shareholders of the firm that gives them the right to use corporate resources only to increase the wealth of those stock-

37. Ibid.
38. Ibid., 181.
39. Ibid., 182.
40. Friedman, *Capitalism and Freedom*, 233.

holders by seeking profits. Executives are not civil servants and have no right under their contract to act on their own preferences, to make discretionary decisions or to expend resources of the firm to achieve social goals that cannot be directly related to profits. Any social action would require a business manager to spend money that was rightfully the property of employees and even customers. According to Friedman no manager can tax the shareholders. If the manager spends the money in a different way than the owners would have spent it, he is in effect imposing taxes, on the one hand, and deciding how the tax proceeds shall be spent, on the other.

A second reason why a manager cannot spend funds for social causes is that insofar as his actions raise the price for the consumer, he is spending customer's money. Insofar as his actions lower the wages of some employees he is spending their money. Therefore, so long as there is corporate tax, there is no justification for permitting deductions for contributions to charitable and educational institutions. Such contributions should be made by the individuals who are the ultimate owners of property in society.[41] People who urge corporations to make charitable contributions are fundamentally working against the economic principle of self-interest and are undermining the basic nature and character of a capitalist society.[42]

An Immanent Ethical Critique

Friedman is correct that, seen from a historical perspective, the capitalist system is a more successful economic system than any other. States that are predominantly welfare states have failed because redistribution underemphasizes achievement and rewards laziness, imposing excessive taxes leads to massive tax evasion, welfarism creates a culture of indebtedness, the funding of unproductive jobs heightens labour costs and a higher standard of living can only be achieved if it corresponds with economic growth. However, the 2008 crisis has also shown that we need a new kind of capitalism with a deeper sense of morality. The neo-liberal version of capitalism that Friedman advocates is for various reasons not the solution.

41. Ibid., 135.
42. Ibid.

The Relationship between Ethics and Economics

A weakness in the neo-liberal version of capitalism is its neglect of ethical issues. Milton Friedman encapsulates the distinction between ethics and economics in terms of normative economics and positive economics, the latter being the true science of economics.[43] Positive economics is, according to Friedman, in principle independent of any particular ethical position or normative judgements. It deals with *what is* and not with *what ought to be* and its performance is judged by the precision, scope, and conformity with experience of the predictions it yields.[44] According to Friedman positive economics can make a better contribution to economics than normative economics because it can be an objective science, in precisely the same way as the physical sciences, and is focussed on making predictions about the economic consequences of certain actions, rather than from fundamental differences in basic values, differences about which men can ultimately only fight.[45] Moral responsibility is an individual matter, not a social matter.[46] Conduct that accords with market criteria is considered as more beneficial by Friedman, than conduct that defies market criteria. Such conduct is considered by him as artificial.

According to Sen, Friedman's method of positive economics has not only shunned normative analysis in economics but it also had the effect of ignoring a variety of complex ethical considerations which affect actual human behaviour.[47] Küng notes that Friedman reduces the whole ethic of the economy to the demand for and promotion of the freedom of the individual.[48] There is no principle for the interaction between individuals, other than the widest freedom possible. Society and the state have nothing to prescribe to the individual. Whether the individual receives his freedom generously or selfishly is irrelevant, as long as he respects the freedom of the other. This methodological and philosophical premise leads Friedman to separate ethics and economics as well as individual and social ethics in a simplistic manner.

43. Rotchild, "Ethics Law and Economics," 123.
44. Friedman, *Essays in Positive Economics*, 4.
45. Ibid., 4–7.
46. Friedman, *Free to Choose*, 135.
47. Sen, *On Ethics and Economics*, 7.
48. Küng, *Global Ethic for Global Politics and Economics*, 191.

All dimensions of life, also economics, need to be subjected to ethical and human criteria for the sake of human beings. The economy is not value-free and it is not only governed by economic laws, but is also determined by the actions of people. Where people operate and make decisions ethical norms and values are at stake. Ethical deliberations can never be totally inconsequential to human behaviour.[49] Even the free market economy cannot escape nor ignore ethical issues because what scholars label as free market forces are actually the outcomes of the playing out of human actions, behaviours and attitudes which are deeply rooted in the quality of human characteristics.[50] Contractual relations that are intrinsic to the operation of the market are themselves grounded in non-contractual shared moral understandings, because legal regulation always needs some social consent based upon a shared moral understanding.[51]

The outcome of a transaction or agreement between two parties also has ethical implications. Though a transaction might be advantageous for the contracting parties, it also might be highly disadvantageous for third parties. It may, for instance, adversely affect the air we breathe, the water we drink, and restrict the natural resources that are available to us. If economics is left mechanically to an impersonal neutral market, third parties might become victims of processes outside of their control. Far from being an instrument of freedom, the impersonal neutral market then becomes an instrument of oppression.

Though Friedman recognises that economic transactions and activities have a neighbourhood effect, he does not sufficiently take into account the real impact of such effects on society. Friedman's answer to the problem of neighbourhood effects is rather precarious. According to him the market provides the most efficacious and expedient solution to economic problems. It assures that only those actions are undertaken for which the benefits exceed the costs, because the exchange process will not be entered into unless there is a perceived potential benefit to be gained. Generally, it is no easier for government to identify the specific persons who are hurt or who benefit than for market participants,

49. See Sen, *On Ethics and Economics*, 4. Kouwenhoven, *Inleiding in de economische ethiek*, 148.

50. Adjidbolosoo, "Quest for Liberalism," 89.

51. Smart, *Economy, Culture and Society*, 108.

and no easier for government to assess the amount of harm or benefit to each.[52]

Smart, however, rightly notes that Friedman answers the question on how the economic activities of a large number of people can be coordinated by generalizing from a model of a simple exchange economy, as if cooperation remains individual and voluntary in a complex enterprise and money exchange economy.[53] The mutual advantageousness of voluntary exchange transactions is obviously correct when applied to two person exchanges, but it is not clear how the voluntary exchange system, if established as the centrepiece in a free market society, provides the key to the promotion of everyone's advantage.[54] Benefit for some does not guarantee benefit for all. Contemporary capitalism is a competitive private enterprise economy that operates in a significantly different manner from a simple exchange economy composed of independent households. Commercial enterprises are much more than benign or neutral intermediaries between individuals in their capacities as suppliers of service and as purchasers of goods. The market must, therefore, be supplemented by regulatory measures that protect the consumer from avaricious sellers and protect society from the spill-over effects of inconsiderate market transactions. Regulation is also needed when some participants are able to control the possessions and goods of a market to such a degree that the market freedom of others is violated.[55]

Friedman's neglect of ethical issues for the sake of a purely economic approach can furthermore be seen in his view that business has no social responsibility except to make profits. Morality is thus reduced to business. Any concern for the well-being of employees, the local community or nation would disturb the natural rational flow of the market and bring artificial elements into the market. In fact, Friedman's economic theory only posits a collection of individuals doing business rationally, united merely by their obligation to freedom.[56] Küng rightly states that such a capitalist business policy destroys the bonds on which a society depends for its continued existence.[57] Shareholders are not the

52. Ibid., 254–55.
53. Ibid., 92.
54. Macleod, "Invisible Hand Arguments," 107.
55. See Smart, *Economy, Culture and Society*, 92.
56. See Küng, *Global Ethic for Global Politics and Economics,* 191.
57. Küng, *Global Ethic for Global Politics and Economics*, 180.

only constituents of a business, there are many stakeholders affected by a corporation's actions.

Friedman's amoral approach to the social responsibility of business also cultivates a culture of greed among business people. The maximisation of profit necessarily will lead to excess, because no moral limits are set for profiteering. If profit is the only concern of a corporation, and if the task to formulate the rules of the game is shifted to government, nothing will constrain the activities of businesspeople because there are no internalised ethical principles on the basis of which business people will act, nor any public interest or common good to serve. Businesspeople will consequently attempt to influence politics in every way possible to see to it that laws serve their own profit seeking interests. The inherent danger of a culture of greed is that more and more of the resources of communities and natural environments are claimed without obliging the individual to contribute more.

Friedman's separation of economics and ethics also has severe consequences for the relationship between the economy and the environment. Environmental degradation is, according to Friedman, acceptable insofar as the benefits exceed the costs to the people involved:

> The real problem is not "eliminating pollution'" but trying to establish rules that will yield the "right" amount of pollution: an amount such that the gain from reducing pollution a bit more just balances the sacrifice of the other good things—houses, shoes, coats and so on—that would have to be given up in order to reduce pollution. If we go farther than that, we sacrifice more than we gain.[58]

The costs of ending pollution entirely are, according to Friedman, excessive, compared to the gains. The best mechanism to respond to pollution is the price mechanism. By imposing a pollution tax the costs born by the community would be transferred to the polluter.[59]

His approach to ecological problems is, however, thoroughly anthropocentric. Nature has, in his thinking, no inherent dignity or value apart from its worth for humans. The problem of the environment is simply approached from the perspective of the benefits and costs for

---

58. Friedman, *Free to Choose*, 257.

59. See Butler, *Milton Friedman*, 217.

people, while the long-term significance of pollution for the environment itself is not taken into account adequately.

The Myth of a Neutral Market

The market is in Friedman's thinking an objective external reality, a mechanism that is central to the allocation of resources in an economy and the primary source of authentication and validation. It is regarded by him as a decentralised, yet organised process of exchange, subject to a general system of law, in which calculating individuals compete, take decisions, enter into transactions and reach agreements.[60] The implication of Friedman's view is that the market process cannot be regarded as subject to moral criticism and that it would be inappropriate to apply criteria of justice to the market process and its outcomes, because such criteria would disturb the immanent rationality of the market. But is the market really an objective system? Does order in the marketplace emerge spontaneously and harmoniously without design or social engineering? What reasonable basis could there be for the expectation that the public interest will be unintentionally served by the uncoordinated economic decisions of individuals if these decisions are based on a mere instrumental conception of rationality such as the pursuit of self-interest?

A fundamental weakness in Friedman's philosophical premise is that he borrows Adam Smith's concept of the invisible hand to support his belief in a neutral market system, but he does this without paying attention to the ethical principles of prudence, justice and benevolence in which Adam Smith embedded his views. Smith underscored values other than self-interest, such as fairness and justice for all, and envisioned economic transactions within an overarching moral framework. He based his ethical code on the virtue of sympathy.[61] Macleod, furthermore, convincingly shows that Friedman gives a wrong interpretation of Adam Smith's argument.[62] Whereas Friedman's understanding of the unintentional goal is that the invisible hand serves to make everyone better off, Smith understood it as maximising the society's gross do-

---

60. See Smart, *Economy, Culture and Society*, 83.

61. See Rothchild, "Ethics Law and Economics," 129. Novak, "Wealth and Virtue," 63.

62. Macleod, "Invisible Hand Arguments," 112.

mestic product. There is, off course, no necessary connection between the two. Friedman also sees voluntary exchange arrangements in a free market society as the reason why the general pursuit of self-interest can promote public interest, whereas Smith, though endorsing the voluntary transactions principle, does not relate it explicitly to the promotion of the public interest.[63]

A further problem with Friedman's understanding of the market is that he simplistically equates the market with coordination through voluntary cooperation. Markets, however, frequently exhibit disorder and produce disorganisation in social and economic life. Smart[64] rightly states that Friedman offers no analytic justification for the equation of the market with voluntary cooperation and the state with coercion. Having choices should not be conflated with having the power or disposition to achieve what you want. The free market economic system has, for instance, come increasingly under the influence of large corporations. The access that consumers have to independent information about goods is, compared to the volume of advertising and the scale of promotions, relatively scarce. Customers don't simply receive what they want. The assumption that everyone ends up satisfied with the outcome of transactions and that everyone obtains what he or she wants seems naïve and ignores the fact that markets are not free from coercion.

Friedman does not consider the issue of how discriminating the exercise of economic strength might be in practice. The idea that economic strength might be employed in such a manner as to erode and undermine democratic political freedoms is not entertained at all. There is no consideration of the possibility that rather than being a precondition for political freedom, the development of capitalist economic life might have other more undesirable political effects. The market form of organisation, for instance, represents one of the most interfering and intrusive influences in people's lives and is increasingly becoming a coercive force to which people are involuntarily exposed.

Friedman's assumption that unlike political power, economic power can be widely dispersed, is also questionable.[65] The reality of economic competition between companies on the one hand and countries

63. Ibid., 116.

64. Smart, *Economy, Culture and Society*, 93.

65. Ibid., 94.

on the other suggests otherwise, as does the fast growing imbalance exemplified by the rising economic and political influence of multi-national companies and the declining economic and political sovereignty of nation states. The global financial crisis that began in 2008 is a clear indication that the market can fail as a regulatory instrument and that there is a need for the implementation of external regulative measures to bring order in the economy.

Freedom and Equality

Friedman assumes that a free market capitalist system fosters freedom and therefore will enhance equality. However, the concept of freedom that he uses is fundamentally flawed, because it is largely negative and procedural in form. Emphasis is placed on the right of the individual to be free of external constraints so that he can be free to choose and pursue his individual self-interest. Autonomy and self-determination lies at the heart of his concept of freedom. Yet for autonomy and self-determination to be realised certain attributes and capacities are needed. In other words, some positive content must be given to freedom. The free market cannot foster the attributes and capacities necessary for the individual to make autonomous decisions. Smart[66] rightly notes that for autonomy to have value non-market institutional spheres, such as the educational, cultural, familial and associative spheres, need to be protected from market forces. Friedman, however, does not restrict free-market logic to the economic system but applies such principles to nearly all spheres of life such as education, health and welfare, thereby either transforming these non-market spheres into commodities that are subject to sale in the market, or more indirectly, by subjecting them to the norms and meanings of the market. In doing so, he neglects the significance of non-market relations for the development of the capacities required to exercise self-determination.

Friedman's concept of equality of opportunity is as flawed as his concept of freedom, because it does not address the crucial question whether the conditions in and through which autonomous agency is to be constituted is fair and favourable. What about those people who do not have equal access to education and jobs because of a lack of resources due to the systemic legacy of political discrimination on the

66. Ibid., 98.

grounds of race or gender? The definition of equality as equality of opportunity will necessarily be detrimental to the social development of such groups of people and will lead to their further marginalisation.

Friedman, furthermore, accentuates the voluntary cooperative nature of the free market system, but underemphasizes the effects that continuous competition has on society. Competition does not always create opportunities, but might also inhibit opportunities, because there are always losers in a competitive environment. Where individuals compete against each other for scarce economic resources, they often attempt to outwit their competitors through methods which are neither fair nor healthy. In fact, the policy of unrestricted market logic advocated by Friedman has led in many cases to rising inequality, poverty and social exclusion, because not all people are able to compete on an equal footing. Interests of people are at times in conflict and not all individuals are equally equipped to protect and promote their interests. The expected benefits from transactions often do not agree with the actual benefits because factors such as a lack of information or incompetence are often present in exchanges. The only way to address the shortcomings in the exchange system is through regulation, something that Friedman opposes fervently.

The global economic system of free trade is currently anything but conducive to greater equality, because there is very limited state intervention and the number of losers therefore far exceeds the number of winners. International corporations have become powerful political forces. In some cases their budgets exceed the gross domestic production of nation states. Third world countries are often exploited by multi-national companies that use cheap labour, dump waste in poor countries, and degrade the environment through unsustainable economic activities. Farmers, entrepreneurs and traders in third world countries find it very difficult to compete with first world countries, because they don't have the same resources as their counterparts in first world countries, and therefore struggle to find markets for their products. In short, the market system alone cannot be relied upon to provide basic needs in respect to food, shelter, health and education. Some kind of distributive justice will always be needed.

Capitalism and Identity

Friedman's preoccupation with autonomy has the potential to give rise to excessive forms of individualism exhibited in the continuous play with identity. Capitalist co-modification leads to a proliferation of increasingly unstable, fluid, shifting and changing identities, because of a constant movement and a perpetual pursuit of innovation.[67] In a sense capitalism continuously attempts to destabilise identity in order to re-establish a new kind of identity that will be open to new products. People's lifestyles need to be adjusted frequently through advertising and campaigning in order to replenish the consumptive capacity of individuals so that new sources of capital income can be accumulated. The condition of being satisfied or contented with one's lifestyle is anathema to a society that requires its members to be actively participating consumers. Consumers are often encouraged to spend more than they can afford on consumption in order to keep the economy operating at a high level.[68]

The excessive importance attached to autonomy and movement in capitalism, furthermore, leads to the erosion of authority. Smart[69] rightly states that where an excessively individualistic form of autonomy gains currency, a tendency towards excessive self-assertiveness is likely to develop, and an unwarranted contrast tends to be drawn between "autonomy" and "authority." There are contexts in which assent to authority is rationally justifiable and consistent with the exercise of autonomy and there are also public domains where an attitude of altruistic service ought to weigh more that the pursuit of self-interest.

The deformation of social institutions is a further consequence of the disproportionate emphasis on movement, continual competition and accumulation that a neo-liberal approach to capitalism brings. Families and communities are, because of the shifting nature of a capitalist society, continuously confronted with the possibility of losing their jobs or losing their businesses. This brings financial and psychological upheaval and causes anxiety and anger.

Friedman's extension of the free market logic into non-market spheres has a profound influence on the traditional roles of profession-

67. Ibid., 100.
68. Ibid., 108.
69. Ibid., 100.

als such as teachers, doctors and academics. In defence of the market, he frequently invokes the idea that the individual should not be constrained by any authority other than his own reason. He thus deploys the potential implications of the coercive use of authority for autonomy as a reason why market forces should be extended to other spheres of life that formerly have been exempted. Friedman assumes that self-interest is the motivating factor, not only in the economic sphere but also in the public sphere and that workers in health care, education and welfare are not motivated by a public service ethos but, as is the case in the private sphere, by self interest and the maximisation of their utilities. An extension of market logic to the public sphere is therefore perfectly legitimate.

Professionals, consequently, become producers, and students and patients become consumers. Heelas and Morris[70] state the matter eloquently:

> The intention is that people will have to exercise initiative, compete for "consumers," cost their activities and think of themselves as "producers," if they are to prosper, let alone retain their jobs. In this fashion, the discipline and rigour of the market helps to construct a mode of selfhood defined in terms of the virtues of enterprise.

The change of identities that free market logic enforces upon professionals necessarily means that projects, activities and research are driven by consumer choices and not necessarily by the interests of the common good. Contrary to the idealistic argument of the invisible hand theorists that consumer choice naturally directs the interests of the common good without willing or knowing it, is the reality that consumer choice and interests of the common good do not always correspond, because there are values that are preconditions for the well being of a society, but that do not necessarily coincide with the preference of the consumer. The ecological crisis is a stark reminder that consumer taste is not an omnipotent force that can be relied upon to serve the common good in all circumstances. In fact, consumerism is one of the major causes of the current ecological crisis that has irreversible global effects on the environment. The same is true with regard to the HIV/Aids pandemic. There is a huge consumer demand for the sex industry, but the financial

70. Heelas and Morris, "Enterprise Culture," 13.

benefit that the sex industry brings for some, is outweighed by its negative effects on the morality and physical health of society.

The identity shift of the professional also has a downside for the client, because the quality of service that a person receives depends upon his ability to afford such services. For instance, the quality of healthcare that a person receives within a strictly free market orientated system is not determined by the scale of his medical need but by his ability to pay for services rendered.

A Christian-Ethical Approach

The 2008 financial crisis is a clear indication that neo-liberalism is not a sound economic doctrine and that capitalism needs to be reformed. The scope of this chapter does not allow for a comprehensive discussion of how capitalism ought to be reformed. I will therefore conclude by identifying some key Christian philosophical notions that will have to be considered if capitalism is to survive.

A Positive Concept of Freedom

It has been noted earlier that Friedman's concept of freedom is largely negative and procedural in nature. Human liberty consists for Friedman in being free from any constraints that are not voluntarily assumed. The result is that he reduces morality to what is profitable and pays virtually no attention to the importance of the common good that transcends the merely profitable. Friedman construes the human being as a *homo economicus* that is inherently self-interested. He therefore approximates human behaviour in economic matters by self-interest maximisation.

However, no economy can function properly if the pursuit of self-interest is the only driving force behind it. The market place needs values that are not self-regarding because the quality of human relationships is crucial to the functioning of an economic system. Self-interested behaviour erodes the social conditions necessary for the sustainability of markets by rendering social relations and commitments precarious and fragile.[71] If the maximisation of profit is the only concern of economics we must be prepared for serious social conflicts and crises. It is clear

---

71. See Hoyt-O'Connor, "Economic Development and the Common Good," 203.

that the principle of freedom ought to be combined with the principle of social equilibrium so that freedom does not undermine social justice.

The Christian understanding of freedom might be helpful in creating a more holistic understanding of freedom that fosters positive human traits. Seen from a Christian perspective, freedom is part of the created structure of the human being, and is therefore an inviolable part of being human. As noted earlier, freedom is, in the Christian view, a positive concept that is always exercised within the framework of justice and love. Positive freedom stresses that the rights of individuals and the community are related concepts and must be balanced in a way that does not violate the dignity of either the individual or the community. Since individual identities are shaped in and through networks of social relations the good of individuals is achieved by promoting the good of their communities.[72] Not all things that are successful in a material sense are therefore morally good.[73] Everybody has a responsibility to respect existing laws, contribute to the common good, consider the impact of his or her actions on the security and welfare of others, to promote equity and to protect the interests of future generations by pursuing sustainable development. Positive freedom counteracts greed and instils in people a sense of moderation and modesty. If the positive dimension of freedom is disregarded, a community will lack a sense of moral responsibility and will succumb to greed and materialism.

Since Christian freedom is essentially a positive concept, it implies a close relationship between freedom and equality, because equality is the positive dimension of freedom. As noted in chapter 6, basic liberties need to be taken for granted and are not subject to political bargaining or to the calculus of social interests. It is, however, not a requirement for a just society that all basic freedoms should be equally provided for. Just social conditions are more important than the right of the individual to enjoy the greatest possible freedom. Rather, freedoms should be adjusted when they clash with each other, so as to provide one coherent scheme equally shared by all members of society. Some freedoms are more essential than others, and more important for a coherent, stable society.

72. Ibid., 208.

73. See Vorster, *Christian Attitude*, 120.

Positive freedom will entail that corporations and business have an obligation towards the common good and therefore must develop the means and the norms to monitor their own actions and to shape themselves as moral agents.[74] The shareholder theory of Friedman that encourages self serving managerial behaviour ought to be replaced with a stakeholder theory that broadens the responsibility of business to appreciate and protect the intrinsic worth of the claims of all legitimate stakeholders.[75] Businesses should be willing, at times, to sacrifice material gain and be satisfied with lower profits and income in order to serve higher ethical goals,[76] the economy must be organised in such a way that it shows social concern for the poor, there must be a symbiosis between business practises and an ethos of human rights, wages must be fair, and the conduct of business ought to be organised in such a way that ecosystems are protected.

Setting Moral Parameters for the Market

Friedman tends to elevate the economic dimension of life above all else by using the free market as a totalised all-encompassing concept. However, there are spheres of social life that need to be protected from market forces, because market relations encroach on more and more areas of modern life and as they do so are transforming more and more social goods (such as science, art, culture and religion) into commodities. The market economy is not an end in itself, it must serve people's needs, not subject them totally to the logic of the market.[77] The Roman Catholic principles of solidarity and subsidiarity and the Neo-Calvinist concepts of sovereignty and universality in own sphere, might be helpful in setting moral parameters for the free market.

The principles of solidarity and subsidiarity are principles of responsibility. Solidarity calls for political and social balance and the furthering of the common good. It articulates the notion that the social and economic spheres of life form an organic whole. Besides individual and personal responsibilities there are also social responsibilities.

74. See ibid., 130.

75. Rothchild, "Ethics Law and Economics," 136. Van Gerwen, "Corporate Culture and Ethics," 55.

76. See Vorster, *Christian Attitude*, 119.

77. Ibid., 211.

Responsibilities, therefore, need to be allocated in such a way that the majority of the members of a community participate in decision-making processes. Applied to economics this would mean that the economic interests of the individual are subject to the general well-being of society. Individuals and corporations ought to take into account the social costs of their economic actions. The common good remains the supreme value and goal of the economy, whereas the market and competition are means and instruments of the economy not goals in themselves.

The principle of subsidiarity states that what individuals can do on their own initiative should not be done by the community, and what the smaller community can do for itself should not be done by the larger community or the state. The value of this principle for economics is that it ascribes a role to the state in the economy, thus legitimising the regulation of economic activities, but it simultaneously limits the role of the state in the economy, by giving it authority to intervene only when all other measures are inadequate.

The Neo-Calvinist concepts of sovereignty in own sphere and universality in own sphere entail that God established a creational order of universal and constant law that governs the different societal spheres. The economic order is thus seen as part of a larger social order. The different societal spheres contain immanent God-given norms that control the processes involved. The creational laws governing social processes are, however, not automatic, but demand human ethical decision-making.

As noted in chapter 6, the principle of sovereignty in its own sphere states that different institutions and associations each have their own intrinsic nature, law of life and area of competence. Whenever a principle valid in one sphere of life, such as bios, or the economic factor, or the aesthetic law of form, is absolutised and imposed upon other spheres, it becomes authoritarian. Neo-liberalism fails precisely in this regard. It applies market logic to non-market spheres.

As stated in chapter 6, the principle of universality in its own sphere expresses the universal coherence of each aspect in its own particular structure. Every sphere has a nuclear moment that has an original meaning for that sphere alone. Yet there are other structural moments, or analogies, in each sphere that point to other legal spheres.[78]

78. See Dooyeweerd, *Encyclopedia of the Science of Law*, 103.

The economic order is therefore related to other spheres of life, but it must not determine other spheres of life by undermining the basic structure and function of such spheres. Market logic must for instance not influence health care in such a way that the quality of health care that a person receives is determined by his financial means and not the extent of his need.

Ecology

The current ecological crisis may lead to bloody wars in future because of the rapid decline in resources. In contrast to economic production, the environment and resources cannot be increased at will. Economics will therefore have to re-orientate itself towards ecological goals and combine economic rationality with a basic ethical orientation.[79] It needs to take account of the social and ecological costs of economic activities to both the present generation and those to come, and it must respect the finitude of the resources upon which it depends and the carrying capacities of the environment and society in which it is embedded.[80]

Neo-liberal economic theory is fundamentally hostile to the environment, because it is in effect a theory of excess that teaches that production, consumption and profit must be maximised through competition in the markets, and is driven by self-interest. However, the philosophy of maximal economical growth can no longer be accepted as morally justified. Rapidly depleting environmental resources and climatic changes are stark reminders that maximum economic growth and human development are not sustainable. Human justice cannot be realized if it does not correspond with ecological justice. Maximal growth philosophy needs therefore to be replaced by a philosophy of efficient economic growth, just distribution of social goods, ecological sustainability and moderate consumption. Efficient economic growth will entail developing clean technology, using renewable energy, promoting consumer preference for products that are environment friendly and using methods such as tracing the carbon footprint and environmental space methods that provide precise guidelines to determine the extent to which consumption levels are exceeding the carrying capacity of the environment in which individual societies live.

79. See Küng, *Global Ethic*, 234.
80. See O'Connor, "Economic Development and the Common Good," 211.

To encourage efficient growth a stricter national regulation of markets as well as a global regulation of markets is needed. Only governments can create and enforce environmental regulations and devise more environmental friendly incentives for markets to respond to.

Conclusion

Neo-liberalism has placed a wedge between business and ethics. This resulted in perpetual gross misconduct in the market place. The 2008 financial crisis was caused by irresponsible lending by banks, overspending by consumers, and an overall culture of greed and selfishness. It is clear that the neo-liberal version of capitalism is too idealistic, simplistic and morally unsophisticated to provide a solution to complex economic issues. The capitalist economic system must be reformed economically, legally and ethically. If not the consequences might be disastrous. We need an organised capitalist system that has regard for the importance of the human relations that underlie all transactions and that takes social justice, equity, fairness and the preservation of the natural environment seriously.

Final Remarks

It is clear from the first part's treatment of the doctrines on evil and original sin that Reformed theology ought to cleanse itself of some of the literalist Augustinian errors that permeate the reformed understanding of creation and sin. If not the theological foundation of reformed anthropology and cosmology will become increasingly untenable because of developments in the natural sciences. The Augustinian notions that the human being was initially an eternal being, that sin is transmitted through sexual concupiscense, and that the original creation was created wholly good without any suffering, simply contradicts established natural scientific facts. Calvin and other reformed theologians have provided some corrections to these Augustinian errors, but the Augustinian legacy still permeates reformed theology. New developments in Old Testament theology on the polemical nature of the creation narratives and the literary genre of these narratives might be helpful in providing a more plausible understanding of the themes of creation and sin. At the same time, the implications of evolution for the Christian faith must not be underestimated. Evolution challenges the Christian faith profoundly on issues such as creation, God's providence and sovereignty, evil and the reconciliation of suffering with God's goodness and omnipotence. However, evolution also contains aspects that point to a divine mystery. Much work still needs to be done within the reformed tradition on the implications of evolution for theology.

Part 2 stressed the need for an integrative approach to the three fundamental human values of dignity, freedom and equality. Human dignity ought to be related to non-human dignity, since human beings are immersed in the natural environment. Contemporary human rights discourse is so engrained in the anthropocentrism of modernity that it discards the importance of the natural environment for human survival. Greater emphasis on third generation rights combined with globally enforced environmental laws will in future be of utmost importance for the maintenance of dignity. It is clear that certain key second and third generation rights should in future enjoy precedence above some first generation rights, such as the right to free trade, freedom of movement, the freedom to practise a profession of your choice, and the freedom to possess private property, in order to protect the environment and natural resources. Global warming and the risks to security that accompany it are the single greatest threat to human dignity today.

Though the protection of freedom is of decisive importance for democracy and social cohesion, it cannot be understood in isolation from the values of dignity and equality. Political liberty, the right to vote, freedom of speech and other freedoms have no significance as long as people have no food to eat or access to natural resources. The growing global inequality is a time bomb that is waiting to explode. It is therefore of utmost importance that liberalism must rethink its stance on the relationship between freedom and equality. Ways must be found to make the values of freedom and equality compatible.

The dangers that excessive freedom and deregulation bring were clearly illustrated in the 2008 economic recession. Capitalism ought to learn from the experience and re-invent itself. We need an organised capitalist system that does not enforce the principles of competition, maximal profit and self interest in all spheres of life, but respects the importance of the human relations that underlie all transactions, that takes social justice, equity, fairness and the preservation of the natural environment seriously.

In the end the human cannot be understood in isolation from his Creator. God, after all, determines the structure, purpose and destiny of the human being. Without due recognition to God's creative actions and His divine will, human relationships lack cohesiveness and equilibrium. Materialist ideologies tend to exhibit elements of one-sidedness, because of their denial of the existence of God and their inclination to absolutise principles in one sphere of life and impose them in other spheres of life. In contrast, the strength of Reformed theological anthropology is that it is able to correlate the values of dignity, equality and freedom with each other because it grounds them, not anthropocentrically in the autonomy of the individual bearer of rights, but within a broad cosmological framework that respects the immanent principles underlying every created sphere of life. Such a cohesive understanding of rights and values is important for a global society that lives on the edge of chaos.

Bibliography

Adjibolosoo, Senyo. "The Quest for Liberalism and Improvements to the Laissez Fair Economic System: The Significance of the Human Factor to Self-Interest." *Review of Human Factor Studies* 9 (2003) 54–103.

Anderson, Bernhardt W. *From Creation to New Creation: Old Testament Perspectives.* Minneapolis: Fortress, 1994.

Anselm. "Cur Deus Homo." In *St. Anselm Basic writings*, edited by S. N. Deane, 191–301. Open Court: Chicago, 1962.

Augustine. *Acta seu Disputatio contra Fortunatum Manicheum 392 AD.* In *Patrologiae Cursus Completus*, edited by J. P Migne. Brepols: Turnhout, 1886.

———. "De Civitate Dei." In *Corpus Christianorum*, Series Latina XLVIII, edited by Bernardus Dombart and Alphonsus Kalb. Brepols: Turnhout, 1955.

———. "De Natura et Gratia." In *Patrologiae Cursus Completus*, edited by J. P. Migne. Brepols: Turnhout, 1886.

———. "De Nuptiis et Concupiscentia." In *Patrologiae Cursus Completus*, edited by J. P. Migne. Brepols: Turnhout, 1886.

———. "De Peccatorum Meritis et Remissione." In *Patrologiae Cursus Completus*, edited by J. P. Migne. Brepols: Turnhout, 1886.

———. "De Perfectione Justitiae Hominis Liber." In *Patrologiae Cursus Completus*, edited by J. P. Migne. Brepols: Turnhout, 1886.

Aulén, Gustav. *Christus Victor: A Historical Study of the Three Main Types of the Idea of Atonement.* 1931. Reprint, SPCK: London, 2010.

Babcock, William S. "Augustine on Sin and Moral Agency." *Journal of Religious Ethics* 16 (1988) 28–56.

Barth, Karl. *Church Dogmatics* III/2: *The Doctrine of Creation.* Edinburgh: T. & T. Clark, 1960.

———. *Kirchliche Dogmatik* III/1: *Die Lehre von der Schöpfung.* Zurich: Evangelischer, 1957.

———. *Kirchliche Dogmatik* III/3: *Die Lehre von der Schöpfung.* Zurich: Evangelischer, 1957.

———. *Kirchliche Dogmatik* II/1: *Die Lehre von Gott.* Zurich: Evangelischer, 1946.

Baskwell, Patrick. "Kuyper and Apartheid. A Revisiting." *Hervormde Teologiese Studies* 62 (2006) 1269–89.

Baumann, Zygmunt. "Modernity, Racism, Extermination." In *Theories of Race and Racism: A reader*, edited by Les Back and John Solomos, 212–29. London: Routledge, 2000.

Baur, Ferdinand C. "Lectures on the History of Christian Dogma." In *Ferdinand Christian Baur on the Writing of Church History*, edited and translated by Peter C. Hodgson. New York: Oxford University Press, 1968.

Bavinck, Herman. *Gereformeerde Dogmatiek.* Deel 3. Kampen: Kok.

Beckley, Harlan, "Empowering Groups and Respect for Individual Dignity: A Review of Michael Walzer's *'Politics and Passion.'"* *Political Theology* (2006) 11–28.

Beeke, Joel R. "The Atonement in Herman Bavinck's Theology." In *The Glory of Atonement: Biblical, Historical and Practical Essays*, edited by Charles E. Hill and Frank A. James III, 324–45. Downers Grove, IL: InterVarsity, 2004.

Berkhof, Hendrikus. *Christian Faith: An Introduction to the Study of Faith*. Rev ed. Grand Rapids: Eerdmans, 1986.

Berkhof, Louis. *Systematic Theology*. Edinburgh: Banner of Truth Trust, 1957.

Berkouwer, Gerhardus C. *Dogmatische Studien: De mens het beeld Gods*. Kampen: Kok, 1957.

———. *Dogmatische Studiën: De voorzienigheid Gods*. Kampen: Kok, 1950.

———. *Sin*. Translated by P. C. Holtrop. Grand Rapids: Eerdmans, 1971.

Bird, Phylis. "Male and Female He Created Them: Gen 1:27 b in the Context of the Priestly Account of Creation." *Harvard Theological Review* 74 (1981) 129–55.

Blocher, Henri. "Biblical Metaphors and the Doctrine of the Atonement." *Journal of the Evangelical Theological Society* 47 (2004) 629–45.

———. The Atonement in John Calvin's Theology." In *The Glory of Atonement: Biblical, Historical and Practical Essays*, edited by Charles E. Hill and Frank A. James III, 279–303. Downers Grove, IL: InterVarsity, 2004.

Bonkovsky, Frederick O. "The German State and Protestant Elites." In *The German Church Struggle and the Holocaust*, edited by Franklin. H. Little et al., 124–48. Detroit: Wayne State University Press, 1974.

Bonner, Gerald. *St Augustine of Hippo: Life and Controversies*. Philadelphia: Westminster, 1963.

Botterweck, Johannes G., and Ringgren Helmer. *Theological Dictionary of the Old Testament*. Vol. 2. Translated by John T. Willis. Grand Rapids: Eerdmans, 1977.

Braulik, Georg. "Deuteronomy and Human Rights." *Skrif en Kerk* 19/2 (1998) 207–29.

Brueggemann, Walter. *Theology of the Old Testament*. Minneapolis: Fortress, 1997.

Brunner, Emile. *Man in Revolt. A Christian Anthropology*. Translated by Olive Wyon. London: Lutterworth, 1939.

Buchanan, James M. "The Matrix of Contractarian Justice." In *Liberty and Equality*, edited by Paul E. Frankel et al., 61–84. Oxford: Basil Blackwell, 1985.

Butler, Eamonn. *Milton Friedman—A Guide to his Economic Thought*. New York: Universe, 1985.

Calvin, John. *Commentaries on the First Book of Moses Called Genesis*. Vol. 1. Translated by John King. Edinburgh: Calvin Translation Society, 1947.

———. *Commentary on the Book of Psalms*. Translated by J. Anderson. Edinburgh: Calvin Translation Society, 1846.

———. *Institutio Christianae Religionis*. Edited by A. Tholuck. London: Berolini, 1846.

Carmichael, Cathie. *Ethnic Cleansing in the Balkans: Nationalism and the Destruction of Tradition*. New York: Routledge, 2002.

Carson, D. A. "Atonement in Romans 3:21–26." In *The Glory of Atonement: Biblical, Historical and Practical Essays*, edited by Charles E. Hill and Frank A. James III, 279–303. Downers Grove: InterVarsity, 2004.

Castles, Stephen. *Ethnicity and Globalisation: From Migrant Worker to Transnational Citizen*. London: Sage, 2000.

Chamberlain, Houston S. *The Foundations of the Nineteenth Century*. Vol. 1. Translated by John Lees. London: Bodley Head, 1913.

Cobb, John B. "Postmodern Christianity in Quest of Eco-Justice." In *After Nature's Revolt*, edited by Dieter T. Hessel, 22–40. Minneapolis: Fortress, 1992.

Crenshaw, Kimberlé. W. "Race, Reform and Retrenchment." In *Theories of Race and Racism: A Reader*, edited by Les Back and John Solomos, 549–62. London: Routledge, 2000.

Davies, Alan. *Infected Christianity: A Study of Modern Racism*. Montreal: McGill-Queen's University Press, 1988.

De Gruchy, John W. *The Church Struggle in South Africa*. Cape Town: David Philip, 1979.

Dooyeweerd, Herman. *Encyclopedia of the Science of Law*. Vol. 1. Translated by Robert. N Knudsen and A. M. Cameron. New York: Edwin Mellen, 2002.

———. *A New Critique of Theoretical Thought*. Vol. 1. Translated by D. H. Freeman and W. S Young. Grand Rapids: Presbyterian & Reformed, 1969.

———. *Roots of Western Culture: Pagan, Secular and Christian Options*. Toronto: Wedge, 1979.

Dreyer, Yolanda. "Vrou as beeld van God. Deel 1: 'n Historiese ondersoek." *Hervormde Teologiese Studies* 56:2–3 (2000) 672–93.

Duffy, Stephen J. "Our Hearts of Darkness: Original Sin Revisited." *Theological Studies* 49 (1988) 597–622.

Du Plessis, Jacobus S. *President Kruger aan die Woord*. Potchefstroom: Pro Rege, 1952.

Duquoc, Christian, "New Approaches to Original Sin." *Cross Currents* (1978) 189–200.

Durand, Jaap. *Skepping, mens en voorsienigheid*. Pretoria: NG Kerkboekhandel, 1982.

Du Toit, Danie. "'n Christelike beskouing van mensregte." *In die Skriflig* 25:4 (1991) 439-456.

Du Toit, Johannes D. *Die godsdienstige grondslag oor ons rassebeleid*. FAK, 1944.

Dworkin, Ronald. *Sovereign Virtue: The Theory and Practice of Equality*. Cambridge: Harvard University Press, 2000.

Ellul, Jacques. *The Theological Foundation of Law*. New York: Seabury Press, 1960.

Eloff, Theuns. *Staatsowerheid en Geregtigheid met Besondere Verwysing na Rasse-klassifikasie: 'n Teologiese–Etiese Studie*. ThD diss., PU for CHE, 1988.

Fichte, Johann G. *Fichtes Reden an die Deutschen Nation*. Berlin: G. Schade, 1908

Frey, Arthur. *Cross and Swastika: The Ordeal of the German Church*. Translated by J. Strathearn Mcnab. London: Student Christian Movement, 1938.

Friedman, Milton. *Capitalism and Freedom*. Chicago: University of Chicago Press, 1962.

———. *Essays in Positive Economics*. Chicago: University of Chicago Press, 1953.

Friedman, Milton, and Rose Friedman. *Free to Choose*. New York: Harcourt Brace Jovanovich, 1980.

———. *Tyranny of the Status Quo*. New York: Harcourt Brace Jovanovich, 1984.

Gaffin, Richard. "Atonement in the Pauline corpus." In *The Glory of Atonement: Biblical, Historical and Practical Essays*, edited by Charles E. Hill and Frank A. James III, 140–63. Downers Grove, IL: InterVarsity, 2004.

Geivett, Douglas R. *Evil and the Evidence of God: The Challenge of John Hick's Theodicy*. Philadelphia: Temple University Press, 1993.

Goldberg, David T. "Racial knowledge." In *Theories of Race and Racism: A Reader*, edited by Les Back and John Solomos, 154–81. London: Routledge, 2000.

Golding, Martin. "'Limited Obligations to Future Generations.'" In *Environmental Ethics: Readings in Theory and Application*, edited by Louis P. Pojman and Paul Pojman, 357–64. Belmont: Thomson Wadsworth, 2001.

Gosai, Hemchand. *Justice, Righteousness and the Social Critique of the Eight Century Prophets*. Theology and Religion. Land Series 7. New York: Peter, 1993.

Grenz, Stanley. "Jesus as the Imago Dei: Image of God, Christology, and the Non-Linear Linearity of Theology." *Journal of the Evangelical Theological Society* 47 (2004) 617–28.

Gustafson, James M. *A Sense of the Divine: The Natural Environment from a Theocentric Perspective*. Cleveland: Pilgrim, 1994.

Haas, Gene. "Kuyper's Legacy for Christian Ethics." *Calvin Theological Journal* 33 (1998) 320–50.

Hannah, John D. "Anselm on the Doctrine of Atonement." *Biblioteca Sacra* (1978) 333–44.

Harland, Peter J. *The Value of Human Life: A Study of the Story of the Flood. Genesis 6–9*. Leiden: Brill, 1996.

Heelas, Paul, and Paul Morris. "Enterprise Culture: Its Values and Value." In *The Values of the Enterprise Culture—The Moral Debate*, edited by Paul Heelas and Paul Morris, 1–27. London: Routledge, 1992.

Herder, Johann G. "Abhandlung über den Ursprung der Sprache." In *Abhandlung über den Ursprung der Sprache: Text, Materialen, Kommentar*, edited by Wolfgang Pross. Reihe Hanser 269. Munich: Hanser, 1978.

Hessel, Dieter. "Eco Justice after Nature's Revolt." In *After Nature's Revolt*, edited by Dieter T. Hessel, 1–21. Minneapolis: Fortress, 1992.

Hettinger, Ned. "Comments on Holmes Rolston's Naturalizing Values." In *Environmental Ethics: Readings in Theory and Application*, edited by Louis P. Pojman and Paul Pojman, 120–23. Belmont: Thomson Wadsworth, 2001.

Hick, John. *Evil and the God of Love*. 2nd ed. London: Macmillan, 1977.

Hitler, Adolf. *Mein Kampf*. Translated by Ralph Manheim. London: Pimlico, 1974.

Hoyt-O'Connor, "Economic Development and the Common Good: Lonergan and Cobb on the Need for a New Paradigm." *Worldviews* 11:2 (2007) 203–25.

James III, Frank A. "The Atonement in Church History." In *The Glory of Atonement: Biblical, Historical and Practical Perspectives*, edited by Charles E. Hill and Frank A. James III, 209–21. Downers Grove, IL: InterVarsity, 2004.

Jenni, Ernst, and Claus Westermann. *Theologisches Handwörterbuch zum alten Testament*. Munich: Kaiser, 1976.

Jónsson, Gunnlaugur. *The Image of God: Genesis 1:26–28 in a Century of Old Testament Research*. Coniectanea Biblica: Old Testament Series 26. Uppsala: Almqist & Wiksell, 1989.

Kinghorn, Johann. "Die groei van 'n teologie. Van sendingbeleid tot verskeiden-heidsteologie." In *Die NG Kerk en Apartheid*, edited by Johann Kinghorn, 86–111. Johannesburg: Macmillan, 1986.

Kirby, W. J. Torrance. "Stoic and Epicurean? Calvin's Dialectical Account of Providence in the Institutes." *International Journal of Systematic Theology* 5 (2003) 309–23.

Kistemaker, Simon J. "Atonement in Hebrews." In *The Glory of Atonement: Biblical, Historical and Practical Perspectives*, edited by Charles E. Hill & Frank A. James III, 163–75. Downers Grove, IL: InterVarsity, 2004.

Kouwenhoven, Arlette. *Inleiding in de economische ethiek.* Nijkerk: G. F. Callenbach, 1989.

Küng, Hans. *A Global Ethic for Global Politics and Economics.* London: SCM, 1997.

Kuyper, Abraham. *Het Calvinisme; zes Stone-lezingen in October 1898 te Princeton gehouden.* 2nd ed. Kampen: Kok, 1925.

Laidler, David. "Milton Friedman—A Brief Obituary." *European Journal History of Economic Thought* 14 (2007) 373–81.

Lohse, Bernhard. *A Short History of Christian Doctrine.* Translated by F. E. Stoeffler. Philadelphia: Fortress, 1978.

Louw, Johannes P., and Eugene A. Nida. *Greek-English Lexicon of the New Testament Based on Semantic Domains.* 2 vols. New York: United Bible Societies, 1988.

Macleod, Alistair M. "Invisible Hand Arguments: Milton Friedman and Adam Smith." *The Journal of Scottish Philosophy* 5:2 (2007) 103–17.

Marshall, P. "Dooyeweerd's Empirical Theory on Rights." In *The Legacy of Herman Dooyeweerd*, edited by C. T. McCintire, 119–43. New York: University Press of America, 1985.

Macdonald, Margaret Y. *Collosians, Ephesians.* Sacra Pagina 17. Minnesota: Liturgical, 2000.

Macdonald, Nathan. "The Imago Dei and Election: Reading Genesis 1:26–28 and Old Testament Scholarship with Karl Barth." *International Journal of Systematic Theology* 10 (2008) 303–27.

Mann, William E. "Augustine on Evil and Original Sin." In *The Cambridge Companion to Augustine*, edited by Eleonore Stumpf and Norman Kretzmann, 40–49. Cambridge: Cambridge University Press, 2001.

Marger, Martin N. *Race and Ethnic Relations: American and Global Perspectives.* 3rd ed. Belmont: Wadsworth, 1994.

Marx, Anthony W. *Making Race and Nation: A Comparison of the United States, South Africa and Brazil.* Cambridge: Cambridge University Press, 1998.

Mathewes, Charles T. "Augustinian Anthropology. Interior Intimo Meo." *Journal of Religious Ethics* 27 (1999) 195–222.

———. *Evil and the Augustinian Tradition.* Cambridge: Cambridge University Press, 2001.

McCormack, Bruce L. "For Us and Our Salvation: Incarnation and Atonement in the Reformed Tradition." *The Greek Orthodox Theological Review* 43 (1993) 281–316.

Meiring, Pieter G. Johannes. "Nationalism in the Dutch Reformed Churches." In *Church and Nationalism in South Africa*, edited by Theo Sundermeier, 56–67. Johannesburg: Ravan, 1975.

Meslé, Robert C. *John Hick's Theodicy: A Process Humanist Critique.* New York: St Martin's, 1991.

Milbank, John. "The Name of Jesus: Incarnation, Atonement, Ecclesiology." *Modern theology* 7 (1991) 311–32.

Miles, Margaret M. "Theology, Anthropology, and the Human Body in Calvin's *Institutes of the Christian Religion.*" *Harvard Theological Review* 74 (1981) 303–23.

Moltmann, Jürgen. *Creating a Just Future: The Politics of Peace and the Ethics of Creation in a Threatened World.* London: SCM, 1988.

———. *God for a Secular Society: The Public Relevance of Theology.* Minneapolis: Fortress, 1999.

———. *God in Creation: A New Theology of Creation and of God the Spirit.* Translated by Margaret Kohl. San Francisco: Harper & Row, 1985.

Nash, John. *Loving Nature: Ecological Integrity and Christian Responsibility.* Nashville: Abingdon, 1993.

Nederduitse Gereformeerde Kerk. *Die NG Kerk in Suid-Afrika en rasseverhoudinge. Opsomming van die belangrikste uitsprake en besluite vanaf 1950-Desember 1960.* Pretoria: NG Kerkboekhandel, 1961.

Nederduitse Gereformeerde Kerk. *Ras, volk en nasie en volkeverhoudinge in die lig van die Skrif.* Kaapstad: NG Kerk Uitgewers, 1975.

Niebuhr, Reinhold. *An Interpretation of Christian Ethics.* London: SCM, 1936.

———. *The Nature and Destiny of Man: A Christian Interpretation.* 2 vols. London: Nisbet, 1941–1943.

Novak, Michael. "Wealth and Virtue: The Development of Christian Economic Teaching." In *The Capitalist Spirit: Towards a Religious Ethic of Wealth Creation,* edited by Peter L. Berger, 51–80. San Francisco: ICS, 1990.

Nozick, Robert. *Anarchy, State and Utopia.* Oxford: Basil Blackwell, 1974.

Pannenberg, Wolfhart. *Anthropology in Theological Perspective.* Translated by Matthew J. O'Connel. London: T. & T. Clark, 2004.

———. "Eternity, Time and Space." *Zygon* 40 (2005) 97–106.

———. *Human Nature, Election and History.* Philadelphia: Westminster, 1977.

Pitkin, Barbara. "'Nothing But Concupiscence': Calvin's Understanding of Sin and the *Via Augustini.*" *Calvin Theological Journal* 34 (1999) 347–69.

Plantinga, Alvin. *The Nature of Necessity.* Oxford: Clarendon, 1974.

Rawls, John. *Political Liberalism.* New York: Columbia University Press, 1993.

———. *A Theory of Justice.* Cambridge: Harvard University Press, 1999

Rees, Geoffrey. "The Anxiety of Inheritance: Reinhold Niebuhr and the Literal Truth of Original Sin." *Journal of Religious Ethics* 31 (2003) 75–99.

Ridderbos, Herman, *De komst van het koninkrijk.* Kampen: Kok, 1950.

———. *Paulus: ontwerp van zijn theologie.* Kampen: Kok, 1966.

Rist, John M. *Augustine.* New York: Cambridge University Press, 1994.

Ritschl, Albrecht. *The Christian Doctrine of Justification and Reconciliation.* Edinburgh: T. & T. Clark, 1902.

Rolston III, Holmes. "Environmental Ethics: Values in and Duties to the Natural World." In *Ecology, Economics, Ethics: The Broken Circle,* edited by F. Herbert Bormann and Stephen R. Kellert, 73–97. New Haven: Yale University Press. 1991.

———. "Naturalising Values. Organisms and Species." In *Environmental Ethics: Readings in Theory and Application,* edited by Louis P. Pojman and Paul Pojman, 107–20. Belmont: Thomson Wadsworth, 2001.

Rothchild, Jonathan. "Ethics, Law and Economics: Legal Regulation of Corporate Responsibility." *Journal of the Society of Christian Ethics* 25 (2005) 123–46.

Santmire, Paul H. "Healing the Protestant Mind: Beyond the Theology of Human Dominion." In *After Nature's Revolt,* edited by Dieter T. Hessel, 57–79. Minneapolis: Fortress, 1992.

Schreiner, Susan E. "Through a Mirror Dimly: Calvin's Sermons on Job." *Calvin Theological Journal* 21 (1986) 175–93.

Schweitzer, Albert. *The Quest of the Historical Jesus*. 3rd ed. Translated by William Montgomery. London: SCM, 1954.

Sen, Amartja. *On Ethics and Economics*. Oxford: Basil Blackwell, 1990.

Smail, Thomas A. "In the Image of the Triune God." *International Journal of Systematic Theology* 5 (2003) 22–31.

Smart, Barry. *Economy, Culture and Society: A Sociological Critique of Neo-Liberalism* Philadelphia: Open University Press, 2003.

Snyman, Gerrie. "Racial Performance and Religious Complicity: Racialised Discourse and Perpetrator Culture." *Scriptura* 90 (2005) 595–607.

Sölle, Dorothee. *Plaatsbekleding: Een hoofstuk theologie na de dood van God*. Vertaling door H. A. Schreuder. Utrecht: Amboboeken, 1966.

Standhartinger, Angela. *Studien zur Entstehungsgeschichte und Intention des Kolloserbriefs*. Brill: Leiden, 1999.

Stannard, Russel. "God in and beyond Space and Time." In *In Whom We Live and Move and Have our Being*, edited by Philip Clayton and Arthur Peacocke, 109–20. Grand Rapids: Eerdmans, 2004.

Staub, Ervin. *The Roots of Evil: The Origins of Genocide and Other Group Violence*. Cambridge: Cambridge University Press, 1989.

Stoker, Henk. G. *Die stryd om die ordes*. Potchefstroom: Calvyn Jubileumfonds, 1941.

Taylor, Simon. *Prelude to Genocide: Nazi Ideology and the Struggle for Power*. London: Duckworth, 1985.

Thielicke, Helmut. *Theological Ethics*. Vol. 1. Translated by William Lazareth. Philadelphia: Fortress, 1966.

———. *Theological Ethics: Politics*. Grand Rapids: Eerdmans, 1969.

Toulmin, Stephen. *The Return to Cosmology: Postmodern Science and the Theology of Nature*. Berkeley: University of California Press, 1982.

Towner, W. Sibley. "Clones of God. Genesis 1:26–28 and the Image of God in the Hebrew Bible." *Interpretation* (2005) 341–56.

Turner, Rachel S. "The 'Rebirth of Liberalism': The Origins of Neo-Liberal Ideology." *Journal of Political Ideologies* 12 (2007) 67–83.

Van Asselt, Willem J. "Christ's Atonement: A Multi-Dimensional Approach." *Calvin Theological Journal* 38 (2003) 52–67.

Van de Beek, Bram. *Jesus Kurios: Christology as Heart of Theology: Speaking of God*. Supplement 1. Studies in Reformed Theology. Zoetemeer: Meinema, 2002.

Van den Berghe, Pierre L. *The Ethnic Phenomenon*. New York: Elsevier, 1981.

Van Gerwen, Jef. "Corporate Culture and Ethics." In *Business Ethics: Broadening the Perspectives*, edited by Johan Verstraeten, 43–78. Leuven: Peeters, 2000.

Vanhoozer, Kevin J. "The Atonement in Postmodernity." In *The Glory of Atonement: Biblical, Historical and Practical Perspectives*, edited by Charles E. Hill and Frank A. James III, 367–405. Downers Grove, IL: InterVarsity, 2004.

Van Wyk, Jan H. "Etiek en menseregte." *In die Skriflig* 21:81(1987) 31–40.

Vischer, Lukas. "Listening to Creation Moaning: Reflections and Notes on Creation Theology." In *Listening to Creation Moaning*, edited by Lukas Vischer. Geneva: John Knox Centre, 2004.

Vogel, Bernhard, et al. *Human Dignity: Christian Responsibility as a Basis for the Practice of Politics*. Berlin: Konrad Adenheuer Foundation, 2007.

Von Rad, Gerhard. *Genesis: A Commentary.* Rev. ed. London: SCM, 1972.

Vorster, Jakobus M. *Ethical Perspectives on Human Rights.* Potchefstroom: PTP, 2004.

Vorster, Nico. "Are Freedom and Equality Natural Enemies? A Christian-Theological Perspective," *Heythrop Journal* 51 (2010) 594–609.

———. "The Augustinian Type of Theodicy: Is It Outdated?" *Journal of Reformed Theology* 5 (2011) 26–48.

———. "Calvin's Modification of Augustine's Doctrine on Original Sin." *In die Skriflig* 44.3 (2010) 71–89.

———. "Christian Theology and Racist Ideology: A Case Study of Nazi Theology and Apartheid Theology." *Journal for the Study of Religions and Ideologies* 7.19 (1998) 144–61.

———. "A Deontological Critique of Milton Friedman's Doctrine on Economics and Freedom." *Journal for the Study of Religions and Ideologies* 9.26 (2010) 163–88.

———. *Kerk en menseregte binne 'n regstaat.* Potchefstroom: PTP, 2003.

———. "Preventing Genocide: The Role of the Church." *The Scottish Journal of Theology* 59 (2006) 375–94.

———. "Relating Human and Non-human Dignity." *Scriptura* 2.104 (2010) 406–16.

Waltke, Bruce, K. "Atonement in Psalm 51." In *The Glory of Atonement: Biblical, Historical and Practical Perspectives,* edited by Charles E. Hill and Frank A. James III, 51–61. Downers Grove, IL: InterVarsity, 2004.

Walzer, Michael. *Spheres of Justice: A Defence of Plurality and Equality.* New York: Basic, 1983.

Webster, John. "Eschatology, Anthropology and Postmodernity." *International Journal of Systematic Theology* 2 (2000) 13–28.

Weinfeld, Moshe. "'Justice and Righteousness': *mishpāṭ* and *ṣedeq*: The Expression of its Meaning." In *Justice and Righteousness: Biblical Themes and their Influence,* edited by Henning G. Reventlow and Yair Hofmann, 228–46. Sheffield: JSOT, 1992.

Welker, Michael. *Creation and Reality.* Minneapolis: Fortress, 1999.

Wentsel, Benjamin. *God en mens verzoend: Godsleer, mensleer en zondeleer. Dogmatiek, deel 3a.* Kampen: Kok, 1987.

Wessels, W. J. "Sosiale geregtigheid: 'n Perspektief uit die Jeremiaboek." *Skrif en Kerk* 13 (1992) 86–90.